13-9: THE STORY OF A GAME, A SEASON, AND A TEAM THAT NEVER QUIT

Chris Peak

13-9: The story of a game, a season, and a team that never quit
Copyright © 2017 by Chris Peak. All Rights Reserved.

Chris Peak
Visit www.panther-lair.com

CONTENTS

PREGAME

The outcome of Pitt's game at West Virginia to close the 2007 season is well-known. Particularly as we approach the 10-year anniversary of that cold night in Morgantown, everyone is aware of what happened:

Pitt, considered to be four-touchdown underdogs with a real chance of losing by twice that amount, put in a performance for the ages, one driven by a whole lot of heart, more than enough toughness, a fair amount of talent and just enough luck to pull off one of the biggest upsets in a season full of unexpected results throughout college football.

But Pitt's win on Dec. 1, 2007, wasn't just a fitting conclusion to an unbelievable regular season in college football. It was the end of an unbelievable regular season for Pitt football. Dave Wannstedt's team encountered every level of absurd twists, mind-boggling decisions, and old-fashioned bad luck that year. It started in training camp and went all the way to the end.

And the fact that Pitt's season ended with an epic upset of the hated Mountaineers almost seemed fitting for the often bizarre events that preceded the game. So while the story of that game has been written in a few places, it's hard to fully grasp what it meant and how big of an impact it had without the context of the whole season.

Because Pitt did more in 2007 than just beat West Virginia. To reduce the Panthers' 2007 season to one game is to miss all the elements that made that game and that win mean so much to the players and coaches who toiled through considerable adversity.

This is the story of 13-9, but it's also the story of the 2007 season. And most of all, it's the story of a team that took blow after blow - some self-inflicted, some not - but never quit. The 2007 Panthers didn't quit on each other and they didn't quit on the season, no matter how many times they found new ways to lose.

That resiliency and dedication is probably why, in the season finale, they didn't lose.

THE SCRIPT

There are no guarantees in sports, and football, with its pointed ball, twenty-two moving parts on every snap, and eight referees making instant decisions on split-second plays that couldn't possibly be seen with the naked eye, is particularly given to unpredictability.

In football, the expected is offset by the unexpected with enough frequency that the unexpected should no longer be a surprise, nor should the expected be viewed with such certainty. Clichés like "any given Sunday" have emerged to reflect the nature of the game, but while those mantras are oft-repeated, there are still those moments when the truly unexpected, the truly unlikely, the virtually impossible still happens.

And when it happens, when the biggest of underdogs upsets the biggest of favorites, the memory doesn't fade quickly. The New York Jets beat the heavily-favored Baltimore Colts in Super Bowl III nearly 50 years ago, and the game is still just as much a reference point in current football discussions as the New York Giants' upset of the New England Patriots 40 years later.

In college football, the separation of divisions - formerly Division I and Division I-A; now Football Bowl Subdivision and Football Championship Subdivision - has created some great upsets. Those upsets have become more commonplace in recent years (there were 10 FCS teams that beat an FBS team in 2016 alone), but perhaps the greatest FCS win of all-time was in 2007, when Appalachian State went to the Big House in Ann Arbor and knocked off No. 5 Michigan.

And yet, somehow that 34-32 win for the Mountaineers would be surpassed three months later as a wild 2007 season wound to its end and unpredictability reigned.

By the final week of the 2007 regular season, the Rich Rodriguez-led West Virginia Mountaineers were the cream of the college football crop. They were 10-1 heading into the finale, a primetime home-field showdown with their rivals, the Pitt Panthers.

Pitt limped into Mountaineer Field that night with a 4-7 record, no passing game and a world of bad luck. West Virginia walked proudly in front of 60,100 fans looking for the ultimate prize: a national championship. The Mountaineers were ranked No. 2 in the nation and had one last hurdle to clear on the path to the title game at the Superdome in New Orleans.

That hurdle was WVU's neighbor to the north - ESPN sideline reporter Holly Rowe called it "very sweet irony" that the Mountaineers needed to win a Backyard Brawl to reach the national championship - and there was little reason to think Pitt would provide any resistance. In the previous two meetings between the long-time rivals, the Mountaineers had humiliated the Panthers' defense, scoring 90 points and putting up more than 1,000 yards of offense. The key was Rodriguez's read-option rushing attack, a scheme that put quarterback Pat White in position to top 200 yards on the ground each year against Pitt in addition to nearly 400 yards from running back Steve Slaton.

The history of the previous two years combined with Pitt's awful performance in 2007 gave everyone confidence in the most likely outcome. WVU believed it would win, its fans certainly believed it would win, and even those who supported Pitt had doubts about the Panthers' chances. Las Vegas set the betting line at four touchdowns in favor of the Mountaineers, and some wondered if that line was too small.

This was WVU's game to win. The 100th edition of the Backyard Brawl would be a blowout, much like the two that had preceded it, and the game would send Pitt into the offseason facing major questions about the direction of its football program.

2007 was Dave Wannstedt's third year as head coach of the Panthers, and somehow the season had gone even worse than his first two. A Pittsburgh native, a Pitt grad and a Western Pennsylvania Guy in every blue-collar, steel-mill-working, mustache-wearing, dialect-drawling sense, Wannstedt had been hired in December of 2004 to replace Walt Harris, the coach who brought Pitt back from its darkest days in the mid-1990's to relevance and a BCS bowl bid.

But Harris never fit in. He gave the fans too many opportunities to point out that he "wasn't from here," too many instances where the Pitt faithful could fall back on vague criticisms like "he doesn't play Pitt football." Wannstedt, by contrast, vowed to do just that when he was hired after Harris left town for Stanford. And the hire brought considerable hype. Pitt fans were excited to have one of their own leading the Panthers, a coach who proudly wore his 1976 national championship ring and spoke of a return to the glory days of Pitt football.

The fan base bought in and the region bought in, and the first nine months of Wannstedt's tenure as head coach floated on a wave of optimism and momentum the program hadn't seen in a long time.

Until they started playing games.

Wannstedt's tenure as Pitt head coach opened in September of 2005 with a Saturday night primetime showdown against Notre Dame at Heinz Field, the Panthers' home on Pittsburgh's North

Shore. The game was Charlie Weis' debut as coach of the Irish, and college football tuned into a national broadcast on ABC to watch Notre Dame, led by quarterback Brady Quinn, walk all over Pitt to the tune of a 42-21 victory.

And that game wasn't even the low point for Pitt in 2005. The next week, the Panthers went to face the Ohio Bobcats on a Friday night and lost in overtime. They didn't win the week after that either, falling to Nebraska. Pitt finally beat Youngstown State in Week Four, but the rest of the season would see the Panthers win just four additional games to finish 5-6, their worst record since 1999 and a fall from the 8-4 mark they posted in 2004.

2006 wasn't much better for Pitt. The Panthers seemed to be on the right track when they opened the season at 6-1, but things fell apart and the team lost the final five games for a 6-6 record and another postseason without a bowl game.

"We were getting better as a program," Wannstedt said in the summer of 2017, 10 years removed from his third season at Pitt. "By that I mean, what the kids were believing, what we were trying to do. But you're judged by wins and losses and there was a lot of frustration, starting with me, that it wasn't happening fast enough. It wasn't happening fast enough. We were just all committed to staying the course.

"I knew how much talent there was there, but God, they were just so young. It takes a few years, you know?"

Wannstedt's 11-12 record at Pitt had slumped to 15-19 by the time the 2007 regular-season finale came around, and despite a contract extension he received the day before the West Virginia game, few saw the program as being on the right track. Wannstedt hadn't returned Pitt to glory; if anything, he was the one leading Pitt's further fall into irrelevance, having wasted the final two years of quarterback Tyler Palko, linebacker H.B. Blades and cornerback

Darrelle Revis - three outstanding players whose careers ended with a pair of bowl-less seasons.

The Panthers had gone from Big East champions and BCS bowl participants the year before his arrival to conference bottom-dwellers, winning six league games total over the 2005 and 2006 seasons. Pitt was losing games and playing uninteresting football, and the miserable nature of the 11 games that preceded the 2007 finale convinced any and all observers that there was really only one likely outcome for that night.

Everything pointed to WVU on December 1, 2007. The night was the Mountaineers', and Pitt would be a hapless participant in their march to a national title. On the ESPN broadcast, singers Perry Farrell and Kelly Rowland collaborated with rapper 50 Cent on a song called "Celebrate," a fitting song for the festive atmosphere that had already begun in Morgantown.

It was 31 degrees, freezing rain was in the forecast, and the West Virginia fans were fired up.

Of course, there are no surprise endings ten years later. Everyone knows that Pitt, led by a valiant running game and an eager defense, upset the mighty Mountaineers on that cold night in December, sending into the night the 60,100 fans and the 100 players and the dozen coaches and the countless cheerleaders, administrators, mascots and other such hangers-on who had already booked their plane tickets to New Orleans.

When the game kicked off, though, the WVU faithful still had their plans in place. Pitt took the ball first, and on the second play of the game, the optimism of the home crowd was further fueled when Pat Bostick, the Panthers' freshman quarterback, was intercepted. It was an auspicious start to the game but, in more than a few ways, the perfect way to commence the final game of what was an unforgettable season for Pitt.

The Panthers ended 2007 on the highest of notes, but the story of Pitt's upset of West Virginia and what it meant for the team and its coach didn't start that night in Morgantown. It began four months earlier and 70 miles away along the banks of the Monongahela River.

A PERSONAL ISSUE

The game that happened on December 1, 2007, is remarkable, and the storylines surrounding that game make Pitt's accomplishment that night even more incredible. But to fully appreciate the 13-9 game requires more than just one night in December, because that game was the culmination of a season that was more challenging than rewarding, a season that saw a team endure more adversity than most seasons bring, a season that ran the gamut of bizarre from the field to the sidelines.

Every game that season had its own speechless moment, it seems. But while those speechless moments took place on and off the field, the first real jaw-dropper of the 2007 season happened a month before the season kicked off as Pitt was opening training camp at its practice facility in Pittsburgh's South Side neighborhood.

That year, the Pitt coaches split the first week of practices in half. Backups and third-teamers would practice in the morning, while starters and freshmen would practice in the afternoon. It wasn't a true two-a-day - the NCAA had limits on those grueling sessions, so each player really only practiced once each day - but the smaller numbers at each practice allowed the coaches more direct work with the players, which was particularly beneficial for the newcomers and inexperienced players on the team.

The first day of practice was Tuesday, August 7. After the morning session, the reporters who covered the team set up in the media workroom to write about the practice they had seen and get ready for the later practice, which would feature starters but also freshmen, who are always of interest.

At the time, the workroom was set up with folding tables placed along the two walls of the room in the southwest corner of the building; the reporters sat at those tables, facing the windows and away from the door that sports information director E.J. Borghetti entered shortly after the first practice.

As Borghetti worked his way through the room, he placed a single sheet of paper in front of each reporter. 10 years later, it's hard to quote the reactions with certainty, but some utterance of shock followed Borghetti's unspoken path around the room.

On the paper was this paragraph from head coach Dave Wannstedt:

"With our full support and understanding, Pat Bostick left campus last night and returned home to Lancaster to deal with a personal issue. Everyone connected with our program has the highest regard for Pat, not only as a talented football player but also as a fine young man. No timetable has been set for his return. We are leaving that judgment to Pat and intend to do everything we can to be supportive of him and his family."

Before training camp even fully started, the star quarterback in Pitt's 2007 recruiting class was gone.

A native of Lancaster, Pa., Bostick had committed to Pitt in May of 2006. Wannstedt was the first coach to offer him a scholarship and quite a few other schools followed suit. Bostick was ranked a four-star recruit on Rivals.com, which also rated him the No. 111 prospect overall in the nation and the No. 6 pro-style quarterback recruit in the class. He had a stat-filled career at Manheim Township High School, and he was expected to be the franchise quarterback for Wannstedt and offensive coordinator Matt Cavanaugh.

"I felt at home, and right after my junior year, I knew where I wanted to go and I wanted to end the process," says Bostick. "That led to me choosing Pitt and I've never looked back."

Except, when Bostick got to Pitt in June of 2007, he did look back. Longingly, he thought about being at home. He thought about the girlfriend at home, the family at home, the friends at home – the *home* at home.

"I left right after my high school prom, got to campus and I had probably as much expectation on me as anybody coming in. You get there and you're coming from farm land and small-town Lancaster County and you're going to Pittsburgh, the big city – it was a wake-up call, you know? I realized pretty quick I wasn't ready yet, and all the emotions you have as a normal kid, I had a harder time handling, for whatever reason.

"It was a challenging summer."

Bostick made it through the summer with weekend trips back home, but when training camp started in August, those trips were about to become a distant memory. Football would be the exclusive focus, and much of the external focus would be on Bostick. He was expected to be the star quarterback. He was expected to lead the team to great success.

He was expected to be the next Dan Marino.

But he wasn't ready for any of that pressure, and on the eve of camp, a few hours after Media Day ended on Monday, August 6, Bostick left.

"I remember sitting in the office one day and he was sitting on the floor and we were talking about everything," Wannstedt says now. "I told him we'd give him a little bit of time and we'd be with him. It was just a lot to deal with."

"I came back home, and I honestly didn't know if I was going to come back to Pitt," Bostick says. "I just was not strong enough at that point to overcome some of those normal feelings, and that, coupled with the external pressure to perform and impress, knowing partially that I wasn't at that level yet – I had hurt my arm and my throwing motion changed my senior year of high school; it was all overuse and over-training and putting too much pressure on myself, and it all came to a head.

"Expectations, reality, what I know of myself – all at a confluence, and I wasn't ready to handle that yet. I needed a kick in the rear end to do it."

Throughout his absence, Bostick's teammates and coaches kept in touch with him. Wannstedt called him every day. Fullback Conredge Collins and quarterback Bill Stull reached out, as did members of the freshman class Bostick had met over the summer. He didn't take most of the calls, partially due to the shame of feeling like he was letting his teammates down and partially because he didn't know if he was going to return to Pitt.

A few days after leaving campus, Bostick attended a high school football kickoff picnic for his brother. Bostick's old coach at Manheim Township was at the picnic, and the coach and the quarterback had a chat. The message was one Bostick had heard from his father and his girlfriend's father: if you end it like this, you'll regret it forever.

The message resonated, and one week after he left Pitt, Pat Bostick was back on the Pennsylvania Turnpike headed west.

"I wouldn't trade that week away," he says. "I needed it personally. When I got back, I was settled into a routine, no one treated me different. I think I proved over time that was just a personal hurdle I had to get over; it wasn't more or less. I wasn't weak-minded or not committed; I had to make a decision for myself, and when I came back, it wasn't like much happened."

One thing that helped ease Bostick back into the team was the quarterback situation. He was expected to be Pitt's next great signal-caller, but not right away. The Panthers were relatively set at the position in August of 2007. Bill Stull was a junior who had seen bits and pieces of action over his first two years while serving as Tyler Palko's primary backup; now it was his turn to be the starting quarterback. And for Stull's backup, Pitt had Kevan Smith, another local product and a redshirt freshman who hadn't played but had good physical tools.

Despite all the pressure and expectations, Bostick took comfort in the fact that he could redshirt in 2007, get settled as a college student-athlete, and look ahead to the coming years.

"Billy had somewhat solidified the starting job, so that pressure was lifted a little bit. It was him and Kevan Smith and I didn't know if I was going to get in there, but I would probably be the third guy. I didn't know if a redshirt was still on the table, but it seemed like the pressure to start right away was off, and I could kind of ease into it a little bit instead of that hot light being on me. Which was good, given the mental state I was in.

"But that didn't last long."

A LOSS IN TWO WINS

Pitt opened the 2007 season against Eastern Michigan in a typical rent-a-win game: EMU came to Heinz Field for a price and with no expectation of Pitt returning the favor with a trip to Ypsilanti, Michigan. It was the kind of game that major college teams schedule, and while Pitt has had more exceptions than most, it seems, it was the kind of game that the host team expects to win.

Eastern Michigan was supposed to be a good warm-up for Pitt. The Panthers entered the season looking for new starters at multiple key positions, from quarterback to several spots on the offensive line and from a few defensive line positions to linebacker and the secondary. Young teams benefit from games against opponents like Eastern Michigan and Grambling, who was on Pitt's schedule for Week Two.

On the first play of the game in the season opener, the youth and inexperience was on full display, but not necessarily in a bad way. When the EMU quarterback threw a pass over the middle, Scott McKillop, a redshirt junior making his first start at middle linebacker, picked up the intended receiver and threw him to the ground in a pile-driver that would likely draw a flag in 2017 football.

But it was 2007, the play was legal, and McKillop announced his presence.

Bill Stull, making his first career start at quarterback, announced his presence as well. He completed his first seven passes in the game, including a 41-yard throw to receiver Marcel Pestano that set up Pitt's first touchdown and a 21-yard touchdown pass to Oderick Turner in the second quarter that put Pitt ahead 14-3.

In between those big passes, another Pitt player made his debut. That offseason, Wannstedt had signed LeSean McCoy, a running back from Bishop McDevitt High School in Harrisburg whose career had been derailed by a devastating ankle injury his senior year. The injury resulted in him attending Milford Academy, a prep school just across the border in upstate New York, and the former five-star recruit who had committed to play at Miami as a member of the recruiting class of 2006 went back on the market as a recruit in the class of 2007.

Wannstedt recruited McCoy before he got to Milford and continued that relationship while McCoy was in prep school, and the diligence paid off when he signed with the Panthers in February of 2007. If Pat Bostick was the star quarterback in Pitt's 2007 recruiting class, McCoy was the overall superstar of the class.

So it was a bit curious when, for Pitt's first three possessions against Eastern Michigan, the superstar recruit didn't see the field. Wannstedt opted to go with LaRod Stephens-Howling, a junior running back who had earned the respect of the coaches and the teammates over the prior two years.

And it was even more curious when Shane Brooks, a little-used fullback/tailback hybrid scored Pitt's two rushing touchdowns in the 2007 opener despite carrying the ball just four times. Stephens-Howling had the most rushing attempts (16 for 67 yards) but McCoy had more rushing yards (68 on 10 carries).

All told, Pitt had a pretty effective rushing attack against Eastern Michigan, while Stull completed 14 of his 20 pass attempts for 177 yards and a touchdown - exactly the kind of clean game Wannstedt was looking for from his quarterback.

But more significant than Stull's stat line was a play he ran on Pitt's second drive of the third quarter. The Panthers were leading 21-3 and Stull had just thrown a 12-yard pass to sophomore tight end Nate Byham that moved the ball to the 50-yard line. On the next play, Stull dropped back to pass but an Eastern Michigan defensive lineman broke through the offensive line and forced him to step up in the pocket. As he stepped up, Stull bumped into Stephens-Howling and was sacked for a one-yard loss.

When Stull huddled with his teammates after the play, he was flexing the thumb on his right hand and continued to flex and shake his hand as the offense approached the line of scrimmage to set up for the next play, a pitch to Stephens-Howling. Stull's apparent thumb discomfort became a full-blown injury when the pitch bounced off Stephens-Howling's helmet and Stull collapsed onto the grass, clutching his thumb in obvious pain.

Stull left the field and was immediately seen by team trainers, but it didn't take a trained medical professional to know that serious damage had occurred.

"It was pretty clear that his thumb was pretty messed up," says Bostick, "so Kevan went in and I had to grab my helmet and be ready to go. It happened like that."

Kevan Smith was Pitt's backup quarterback, and his collegiate debut consisted of him throwing four passes and completing two of them for 18 yards. Wannstedt didn't make anything official regarding Stull's status in his postgame press conference, but Stull had surgery to repair a torn ligament in his thumb the day after the game, ending his season.

"God, that was just crippling," says Wannstedt, "because he was going to be the starter and when he got hurt - we had three guys that had no experience and then he got hurt and now we had freshmen and sophomores."

A week later, Pitt hosted Grambling State at Heinz Field, and Smith was the starting quarterback. It was a rainy day, perfect for the kind of sloppy performances both teams would put in. Pitt and Grambling combined for 24 penalties and seven turnovers; they both struggled with the wet, muddy grass at Heinz Field; they both even attempted ill-fated double-reverse handoffs on their first possessions of the game, gaining a combined total of minus-14 yards in the process.

Smith was mostly efficient and largely unspectacular in his first collegiate start, completing 15-of-22 passes for 202 yards, one touchdown and one interception. But the star of the show was McCoy; the freshman running back didn't start, but he appeared on Pitt's second possession and had 47 yards on that drive - 30 rushing, 17 receiving - including his first touchdown in a Pitt uniform, a five-yard run to give the Panthers a 7-0 lead.

Pitt got the ball back at the Grambling 7-yard line after walk-on linebacker Brian Kaiser blocked a punt, and McCoy punched it in on the first play. He made it three-touchdowns-in-three-plays on the next drive when he was inserted for a first down at the Grambling 13 and ran to the end zone.

After a debut that was rather unexciting the previous week against Eastern Michigan, McCoy opened the Grambling game with 50 yards and three touchdowns on four rushing attempts. By the end of the game, McCoy had 107 yards and the trio of scores on 19 carries - the first of his 13 100-yard games at Pitt.

McCoy's breakout was the big storyline for the Panthers, but it was hard to miss the other side of the ball. Pitt's defense held Grambling to 239 yards of total offense, forcing five punts, three interceptions and three turnovers on downs - effectively killing 11 of the Tigers' 13 possessions. That picked up a trend from the

Eastern Michigan game, when Pitt had allowed just one first down in the second half and forced the Eagles to punt on three-and-out drives on four of the five second-half possessions.

2005 and 2006 had been miserable for the Panthers' defense as Wannstedt struggled to find the personnel that fit what he wanted to do, but McKillop and a young-but-improving defensive line were showing signs that 2007 could be different. They were still inexperienced, but the potential was on display.

Pitt rolled to a 34-10 win over Grambling that day, but before the Panthers could stroll victoriously to the locker room, there was one more debut to make. With the game in hand and about 12 minutes left in the fourth quarter, Wannstedt decided it was time to put the freshman quarterback in the game. Since Stull was out for the season, Bostick was now the backup, and there are few things coaches fear more than a quarterback taking the field with zero experience. So he gave Bostick the proverbial tap on the shoulder and sent him in.

"I knew I was going to get some snaps, probably in the fourth quarter," Bostick says. "And my first snap was not the best."

The drive started out okay. A four-yard run from McCoy, a five-yard penalty on Grambling and a four-yard run by Shane Brooks picked up a first down. On second-and-10 from the Pitt 17, Bostick dropped back to attempt his first collegiate pass - and threw it right into the belly of Grambling linebacker John Carter.

"I was pretty nervous; it was my first time out there," Bostick says. "I wanted to throw the inside slant on two slants; outside being a longer throw and the inside being a quicker throw and something that, even if it was end over end, it could still be completed. That was a poor decision and I completely telegraphed it. The linebacker I thought was going to go outside, did go outside. But I didn't see the next linebacker in the middle, who read my eyes and just jumped right in front of it.

"What a knock-you-down-to-size moment. Then again, you get everybody telling you that Dan Marino threw a pick on his first pass. But I didn't throw a touchdown on the play after that. Then you start wondering if you can even play at this level."

Bostick's second drive ended with a punt, but his third drive was ideal: two handoffs to Brooks to kill the remaining time on the clock.

Pitt had lost its starting quarterback, but the Panthers were 2-0 and ready to head west to take on an opponent from the Big Ten - and they had something special up their sleeve.

INTERCEPTION, PUNT, PUNT

Pat Bostick's interception on his first pass attempt in college could be chalked up to nerves and inexperience. By the time the regular-season finale rolled around three months later, Bostick had calmed his nerves and gained some experience, so he had neither of those excuses when his first pass attempt at West Virginia was picked off.

The pass was a first-down throw from the Pitt 45 to receiver Oderick Turner on the right sideline, but it was underthrown and WVU cornerback Antonio Lewis got in position to intercept it. A home crowd that was already raucous grew even more so after the pick, as the game's inevitable outcome seemed to be playing out as expected after just two snaps.

Bostick and the offense went to the sideline after the interception and the West Virginia offense, led by the dynamic Pat White, came out for what was likely to be the first of many successful drives. The Mountaineers had no shortage of playmakers around White - running back Steve Slaton was a future pro, all-purpose weapon Noel Devine was a Deion Sanders pupil and a super star, even fullback Owen Schmitt was a handy tool in the box for WVU as a bruising punisher with or without the ball in his hands.

Lewis' interception return had set up the WVU offense at the Pitt 27-yard line, but it was Schmitt who really moved the Mountaineers closer to the end zone, busting off a 12-yard run on third-and-3 that took an already-electric crowd and made it even louder, rowdier, and crazier.

Everything was going according to the script: Pitt's offense was terrible and mistake-prone and West Virginia's running game was marching to the end zone. Except the Panthers' defense fought back, stopping Devine for a one-yard loss, corralling White after three yards, and then covering well on a third-down roll-out as White looked for a pass option.

White tried to scramble for the goal line, but linebacker Jemeel Brady, making his first career start in a different look for Pitt's defense, got him out of bounds short of the end zone.

No matter, the WVU faithful figured; the offense might not have scored a touchdown on this drive, but there will be plenty more opportunities to score in seven-point increments. In the meantime, the home crowd expected kicker Pat McAfee to get the game's first points on the board with a 20-yard chip shot field goal attempt.

But McAfee hooked the kick, missing the goal posts to the left and leaving WVU scoreless. On one sideline, ESPN's cameras caught WVU head coach Rich Rodriguez mouthing, "What the heck?" On the other sideline, the cameras captured an energized Dave Wannstedt issuing a pair of fist pumps.

Wannstedt had extra reason for celebration after the missed field goal. McAfee was lined up on the left hash mark, and while the distance of the kick - 20 yards - wasn't a challenge, the angle was. Close-range kicks from either hash mark can be tricky for a kicker, so before the kick, WVU had tried to take a delay of game penalty that would have moved the ball back five yards and given McAfee some extra space and a better angle on the goal posts.

But Wannstedt declined the penalty, taking his first chance of the game. And it paid off when McAfee missed.

Pitt's offense didn't capitalize on the missed field goal, as WVU swarmed around LeSean McCoy on every snap and a screen pass from Bostick to receiver T.J. Porter was off the mark and only catchable if Porter laid on the ground (which he did).

For the second consecutive drive, though, Pitt's defense was ready to cover for the offense. On a second-down play, White ran to his right with Slaton as the pitch option if that's what the defense forced, but he didn't expect Pitt defensive end Joe Clermond to close on him so quickly. Clermond got to White fast and forced a bad pitch that lost five yards. And on the next play, linebacker Scott McKillop tackled receiver Jock Sanders on a flanker screen after just four yards.

A three-and-out? From WVU's powerhouse offense? That wasn't the script. The Mountaineers had scored 66 points the previous week against Connecticut, the second time in the season they topped 60 points, the third time they scored at least 50, and the fifth time they managed 40 points. Plus, against Pitt in the past, they had been unstoppable. Now they were looking at one first down and no points from their first two drives. That wasn't how things were supposed to go.

Fortunately for the home team, their visitors were still playing the part. A pair of McCoy runs on the next drive gained six yards, but Bostick was sacked for a five-yard loss on third down, and Pitt was punting again.

That was a theme that had defined Pitt all season: poor, ineffective play from the passing game and solid, churning work from McCoy. Bostick had one completion for zero yards, an interception and a five-yard sack on the first three drives; McCoy had 21 yards on his first five rushing attempts.

When good things happened for Pitt in 2007, they usually happened because of McCoy. He was the engine for the Panthers, an outstanding talent who would have been a star at any college. And he almost played his college football in a lot warmer climate.

SHADY

In the summer of 2005, there weren't many high school football players who were better than LeSean McCoy.

That's not hyperbole. That May, Rivals.com released its initial ranking of five-star prospects in the 2006 recruiting class - the cream of the crop - and McCoy was No. 4 on the list. No running back in the nation was ranked higher than him, and for good reason: as a junior at Bishop McDevitt High School in Harrisburg, he was a bona fide superstar.

"I knew him since high school," Pat Bostick says. "We scrimmaged them every year, and I remember when we went up there my junior year. They were going to be all-world at that point...and he played two plays against us in that scrimmage: the first play was a 14-yard toss sweep and the second one was a 64-yard screen for a touchdown. And he was done for the day.

"I remember seeing him later walking around, talking to all girls and everybody, wearing his Superman cut-off shirt that he always wore. And I'm like, 'That dude has some sauce to him. There's no doubt he's the best player I've ever seen.' I never thought our paths would cross again."

Through three years of his high school career to that point, McCoy had rushed for 5,781 yards and 65 touchdowns, and he opened his senior year looking like he was on the same track, rushing for 300 yards in one game and topping 200 in another. But his senior stats ended at 859 yards and 10 touchdowns when, in the fourth game of the season, McCoy suffered a compound fracture in his ankle.

The injury immediately ended his season and his high school career, but it also derailed more than that. By his own admission, the injury and the subsequent surgery left McCoy depressed. He slipped on his schoolwork, and while he announced on National Letter of Intent Signing Day in February of 2006 that he intended to sign with Miami, it was generally understood that he wasn't going to be going to a Division I college that summer on account of his grades.

Instead, his poor academics led him to Milford Academy in New Berlin, New York. A home for wayward athletes whose grades aren't good enough to get into Division I schools, Milford counts more than 30 former players who were on NFL rosters in the 2017 season.

So that was McCoy's destination. He joined a roster that also featured Graig Cooper, another Miami running back recruit who also didn't make grades. And for most of the season, McCoy, the former five-star recruit and No. 1 running back in the nation, was behind Cooper on the depth chart.

"It was sad," Dave Wannstedt says. "I remember going up to Milford Academy with David Walker and LeSean McCoy was second-team running back at a prep school and he was still limping. And it was like the middle of October. It damn near brought tears to my eyes. Because, to this day, he's the best high school prospect I ever watched on tape.

"I mean, his high school tape was off the charts. You don't see first-round draft pick tape that was as impressive as his; he was running, catching, making people miss, doing everything, and that was going into his senior year."

Milford wasn't Wannstedt's first interaction with McCoy. The summer before his senior year at Bishop McDevitt, McCoy and a few teammates (including cornerback Aaron Berry, who ultimately signed with Pitt) visited the Panthers during a training camp practice. The coach and the running back made a good connection that day, but it didn't matter much; McCoy's list of interested colleges spanned from coast to coast, and he had his eye on programs like Miami, USC, Penn State, Florida, and more.

After the injury and the detour to prep school, McCoy took a different view of Pitt. For a period of time in the fall of 2006, he still maintained his commitment to Miami. But by the time the calendar year changed, it was clear that Pitt was at the top of his list, and in February of 2007, he signed with the Panthers.

"When he got hurt, I was still recruiting Aaron Berry so I was spending a lot of time up there and I got to know his family some," says Wannstedt. "So when I went by the school, I was just encouraging him because everyone at the school was telling me he was so down in the dumps. He thought his football career was over. So I was just up there to try to encourage him.

"We stuck with him and I think the reason he came to us is that I made a commitment to him and his mother that he had a scholarship at Pitt. And I'll be honest with you: I didn't know if he was going to recover or not or get back to full speed. I really didn't know. I just developed some strong feelings toward the guy as a person as well as a football player."

Wannstedt may have been uncertain about McCoy's recovery, but it didn't take long for the talent to show up. McCoy was Pitt's best player from the start of his first practice with the Panthers, and while he got limited opportunities in the first two games of his freshman season, he still averaged six yards per carry and scored three touchdowns.

It was enough that, in the lead-up to Pitt's Week Three game against Michigan State, Andre Ware, who served as color commentator on the game, predicted that McCoy would "have his coming-out party," adding that "the nation will get to see why he was so highly-recruited coming out of high school."

Ware called McCoy a "special, special talent," and the freshman from Harrisburg by way of New Berlin would prove him right - and then some.

ARKANSAS GIVES, ARKANSAS TAKES

Before the Michigan State game kicked off, though, Pitt experienced some more attrition.

This wasn't a season-ending injury for the football team - although there would be plenty of those - but rather it was on the administrative side. Jeff Long, who had served as Pitt's Athletic Director since 2003, was announced on September 11 as the new A.D. at Arkansas.

Wannstedt still remembers when Long, who had hired him 33 months earlier, told him he was leaving for the Razorbacks and the Southeastern Conference.

"He came up to my room and it was a very emotional meeting," Wannstedt says. "I knew (Pitt Chancellor) Mark Nordenberg for a long time and I really thought that he was committed to what we were doing, but the real reason I took that job was because of Jeff Long.

"Jeff knew football and he was an athletic director, but he and I had a plan over the next ten years to get Pitt back to competing for championships. But Arkansas tripled his salary and gave him a Learjet and everything else that went in that package. I remember in the hotel room, I gave him a hug and said, 'You know Jeff, you've got to take that job. That's a great opportunity. Good luck to you.'"

Long's departure for Arkansas opened a vacancy in Pitt's Athletic Department that would initially be filled on an interim basis by long-time administrator Donna Sanft - a move Wannstedt whole-heartedly endorsed; he would view the hire that ultimately replaced Long two months later less favorably - but Wannstedt didn't have much time to bemoan the professional loss of a friend and a boss.

After winning its two season-opening games at home against lower-level competition, Pitt had to go on the road in Week Three to face Michigan State from the Big Ten. The Spartans were in a transition of their own; Mark Dantonio, who had faced Pitt as the head coach at Cincinnati the previous two years, was now leading the MSU program.

Like Pitt, MSU had opened 2007 with relatively easy wins over UAB and Bowling Green, and the Panthers presented the Spartans with their first test of the season. A year earlier, MSU had come to Heinz Field and ran roughshod over Pitt, winning 38-23 in a game that wasn't even that close. The 2007 Spartans had a talented team, with future NFL players at quarterback (Brian Hoyer), running back (Javon Ringer), and wide receiver (Devin Thomas), among others, and they would go 7-5 in the regular season.

On defense, MSU had allowed just 59 rushing yards in its first two games - a number that ran counter to what Pitt hoped to do in its trip to East Lansing. With Kevan Smith set to make his first career road start, the Panthers needed to rely on the run game more than ever.

There was another problem. While McCoy was fresh off his first career 100-yard rushing performance, Wannstedt and his staff hoped to deploy a ground game that relied on multiple players. But junior back LaRod Stephens-Howling, who started the first two games and made for a nice alternative when McCoy needed a break, had injured his ribs the previous week and was not available at

Michigan State. Nor was sophomore Kevin Collier, who dislocated his wrist in training camp.

So when Pitt landed in East Lansing the Friday before the game, the running back corps consisted of McCoy and freshman Greg Williams; the coaches had no intention of playing Williams and even planned to move him to linebacker - he would eventually end spend the bulk of his Pitt career there - so the plan was clear:

There would be no substitutions. As long as McCoy was healthy, he would be on the field.

It didn't take long for McCoy to prove that he was, in fact, Pitt's best chance at winning that afternoon. After Smith threw an interception in the first quarter that led to a touchdown run by Michigan State's Jehuu Caulcrick, McCoy answered right back. On the first play after the Spartans' touchdown, Smith faked an end-around handoff to freshman receiver Maurice Williams and gave the ball to McCoy, who found a hole in the middle of the defense and then used his speed to bolt 64 yards down the field for a touchdown.

The tie score didn't last long, though. Pitt's defense did its part when a sack by defensive tackle Mick Williams forced a punt, but on the third play of the Panthers' next possession, Smith was intercepted again. This time, the turnover led to a touchdown much more quickly; the pass was supposed to be a screen to receiver Oderick Turner, but it was off the mark and Turner tipped it right into the arms of MSU safety Travis Key, who ran 31 yards to the end zone.

At that point, Smith had completed more passes to Michigan State players than Pitt players, and the theme continued throughout the first half: Pitt's offense kept sputtering and Pitt's defense kept stepping up.

The final drive of the second quarter seemed to perfectly sum up the day to that point. Pitt's defense gave the ball back to the offense at its own 23 with 44 seconds left to play. On first down, Smith threw to tight end Darrell Strong for 13 yards and on second down, he hit receiver T.J. Porter for 15 more yards. In a matter of two plays, the Panthers were getting close to field-goal range with 28 seconds on the clock.

But Smith scrambled on first down from the MSU 48 and then, after back-to-back false start penalties on Pitt offensive linemen, the Spartans defense sacked Smith in the backfield for a 10-yard loss. A once-promising drive blew up in Pitt's face, and the Panthers went to halftime in disarray. They had a surprise waiting for the second half, though.

In the time between the 2006 and 2007 seasons, Wannstedt sent offensive coordinator Matt Cavanaugh on a mission.

Wannstedt, like the rest of the nation, had noticed something at the University of Arkansas the previous year. The Razorbacks, under head coach Houston Nutt and offensive coordinator Gus Malzahn, had two great running backs but instability at quarterback. So rather than attempt 300 passes in 2006 - even Pitt, with Wannstedt's run-heavy emphasis on offense, had thrown more than 330 that season - Arkansas turned to its running backs in a fairly direct manner.

Nutt and Malzahn called it the "Wild Hog" formation, and it featured those running backs, Darren McFadden and Felix Jones, taking a direct snap from the center. From there, they would either run with it, hand it off to a wide receiver who ran in motion across the formation or, on seven instances, throw the ball. The offensive approach was born in the 1950's but South Carolina head coach Steve Spurrier had rebirthed it in 2005 and Malzahn, who came to Arkansas from the high school ranks, perfected it with the Razorbacks.

Get the ball in the hands of your best player, the thinking went, and Wannstedt, knowing he had talent at running back but uncertainty at quarterback wanted some of that for Pitt. Cavanaugh and the Panthers' offensive coaching staff came up with a package of plays where the ball was snapped directly to McCoy or Stephens-Howling; a wide receiver would run in motion across the formation prior to the snap and could take a handoff from McCoy or Stephens-Howling to run an end-around, but on most plays, the running back kept it.

"Houston Nutt was the quarterback at Oklahoma State when I coached there, so I sent Matt Cavanaugh down there and he came back with four or five plays," Wannstedt says. "It was more of a situation of, how could we get the ball to LeSean? It was a way to get the ball to some playmakers that gave us more opportunity to make some plays.

"Really, the plan was, we had freshmen and sophomores at quarterback who hadn't started before. So I knew, from a quarterback standpoint, that we weren't going to be able to line up and throw the ball like when we had (three-year starter) Tyler Palko. It was a situation where we were going to have to do something."

Pitt didn't show the new offensive look - they called it the "Wildcat" - through the first two and a half games of the 2007 season. But after the first half at Michigan State, Wannstedt had no choice. Smith was struggling mightily, completing 5-of-9 passes for just 32 yards and two interceptions through the first two quarters; his first seven pass attempts in the game gained a total of four yards.

In his halftime interview, Wannstedt said that a decision on changing quarterbacks from Smith to Pat Bostick "is yet to come."

On the broadcast, color commentator Andre Ware was not so hedging.

"Dave Wannstedt, Matt Cavanaugh, they're doing more damage to this kid's psyche," he said, referring to Smith's obvious struggles.

On the first play of the second half, Smith was on the field but he wasn't lined up at quarterback. He was at wide receiver and McCoy was in the backfield for the debut of the Wildcat. Michigan State's defense wasn't ready for it, and McCoy took the direct snap eight yards on first down, picked up three yards on second down and then handed the ball to receiver T.J. Porter on an end-around out of the Wildcat for another nine yards.

The new package was working, but it couldn't do everything, and when Pitt had to throw again, a Smith pass on third-and-3 was dropped by tight end Darrell Strong. The Panthers went back to the Wildcat on their next drive and McCoy led the offense to a field goal to cut Michigan State's lead to 14-10. As the game continued, Pitt's defense kept stopping Michigan State's offense, keeping the Panthers close enough to have a chance to win.

It looked like Pitt would put itself ahead of MSU when, in the fourth quarter, Porter broke a 31-yard run out of the Wildcat that turned into a 46-yard gain after a 15-yard facemask penalty was added at the end of the run to put the Panthers inside the Spartans' 20-yard line. From there, McCoy ran twice to get to the MSU 8, and a go-ahead touchdown - possibly the game-winning touchdown - was in reach. But center Chris Vangas was flagged for a facemask penalty on first down from the 8, which moved the ball all the way back to the MSU 23, a huge loss of yardage for an offense that needed all the help it could get. Three plays later, Pitt was settling for a field goal from placekicker Conor Lee; the kick was successful, but Pitt still trailed 14-13.

Pitt's hopes were dealt one more blow - by the Panthers' offense, no less - when the team's defense stopped MSU one more time late in the fourth quarter. On first down, Porter took a handoff from McCoy out of the Wildcat but fumbled and Michigan State recovered. The Spartans got a field goal out of the ensuing drive to pad their lead, but at that point it didn't matter: Pitt's offense wasn't going to catch Michigan State, not on that afternoon.

The Panthers had a chance against a Big Ten opponent on the road, an opportunity to get a serious confidence boost for a young team that was still trying to figure itself out. Instead, Pitt suffered a heartbreaking loss, but there was at least some cause for optimism. The Panthers' young defense was playing well; linebacker Scott McKillop had 17 tackles in East Lansing that afternoon and Pitt held MSU to 360 yards of offense and just one touchdown. Plus, McCoy had broken out in a big way, rushing 25 times for 172 yards and a score.

With what looked like the makings of a really effective defense and a very strong running game, Pitt just needed to get the quarterback situation figured out; if that could be resolved, the Panthers just might have a chance to be pretty good in 2007.

READY TO FIGHT

Pat Bostick had been intercepted on his first pass against West Virginia in the 2007 regular-season finale, and the next two drives didn't produce more. The Panthers punted on each of those two possessions, and after three drives, they had run eight plays and gained 16 yards - 12 of which came of McCoy's run on the first play of the game.

At the end of that 12-yard run on the first play, though, something happened with Pitt left tackle Jeff Otah and West Virginia defensive end Johnny Dingle. Otah was a second-year player at Pitt, a junior-college transfer from Valley Forge Military Academy who had been a starter for both of his seasons with the Panthers. He had played in one game against WVU the previous season, but he was originally from Delaware, so he didn't have a lot of context for the Backyard Brawl.

But on the first play of the game, Otah went right at Dingle, a second-team All-Big East player and one of the Mountaineers' best defenders.

"Jeff Otah was a JC transfer; he knew nothing about this rivalry," Dave Wannstedt says. "But the first play of the game, he came off the ball against their big defensive end, who was a great player, too, and those two guys hit, it was like two rams hitting face-to-face. And boy, the play didn't end there. They got after each other and started wailing each other and flags started flying.

"That's one thing about me, to a fault: players knew where I stood. In my days at Pitt, I didn't have any drug problems, I didn't have any rape problems, I didn't have any theft problems; but what we had was, we had our share of bar fights. And that's wrong, too; that's not what I'm saying. But the players always knew where I stood on that, because that's how it was when I played there and that's what Pitt was about, you know?

"So flags started flying and I remember players on the sideline looked at me to see how I was going to react with Jeff because I told them, 'We can't afford to give them anything penalty-wise.' And, shit, I didn't say anything; they knew that 'That's what this is about, guys. Let's go.'"

Otah and Dingle were both flagged for unsportsmanlike conduct penalties on the play, and since the flags offset, McCoy's 12-yard run stood. Otah didn't get an earful from Wannstedt after the play, and neither did tight end Darrell Strong, who had a similar altercation with WVU defensive back Vaughn Rivers after a play on Pitt's second possession. Once again, the referees called a pair of offsetting unsportsmanlike conduct penalties, so there was no harm to Pitt from Strong mixing it up with Rivers.

But maybe what showed on those plays was that West Virginia, with the No. 2 ranking and the potent offense and everything to play for, might have been wound a little too tight. The Panthers seemed to be in the Mountaineers' heads a little, baiting the home team into penalties and maybe, just maybe, gaining a bit of a psychological edge.

"That's what we went down there with," Wannstedt says. "I think the guys knew that, a penalty for jumping offsides or a penalty for whatever else, I'm going to get upset with. But as far as mixing it up with these guys, that's what that game's about. It's the Backyard Brawl, you know?"

Of course, it didn't help when West Virginia's vaunted offense, which had scored touchdowns on its first two possessions against Pitt the year before, was having trouble getting rolling. After missing a field goal on its first drive and punting on its second, the Mountaineers were getting a bit antsy for points on their third try. A 21-yard run by quarterback Pat White moved the ball deep into Pitt territory and bruising fullback Owen Schmitt pounded his way for a first down inside the 20.

But a great tackle by Pitt cornerback Aaron Berry led to a third-and-6 for WVU; then White rolled out and tried to throw to receiver Darius Reynaud, but he had to hurry the throw because Pitt safety Eric Thatcher was headed right for him. White got the worst of it: the pass was incomplete *and* he took a shot from Thatcher.

Pat McAfee, the WVU kicker, came out after the incomplete pass to attempt a 32-yard field goal. But for the second time in the game, McAfee, who had a 70% career success rate and would finish his time at WVU making 17-of-20 (85%) kicks in his senior season, missed. And as the first quarter drew to a close, Pitt and West Virginia were dead-locked in a scoreless game.

BOOS AT HOME

When Pitt lost to Michigan State in Week Three of the 2007 season, it wasn't quite a moral victory, but it was an encouraging loss. LeSean McCoy had announced his presence as a superstar. Pitt's defense had played a very tough game and looked like it was coming into its own. And, most of all, the Panthers had hung in against a Big Ten opponent on the road, battling for 60 minutes and coming up just short at the end.

If they could make one or two more plays, they might have a chance to put together a few wins in a row. They just had to keep battling.

Less than two minutes into Pitt's next game, that optimism was lost.

The opponent for Pitt the week after the Michigan State game was Connecticut, a Big East opponent that still felt new as a conference foe, at least in football. The Huskies had joined the Big East for football in 2004 - they were a founding member of the league for basketball - but while they hadn't been in the conference as a football entity for four full seasons yet, they had stung Pitt a few times.

In 2004, the Walt Harris-led Panthers went to East Hartford and lost in a game that accelerated Harris' departure later that season. Dave Wannstedt beat UConn in his first season, but he suffered the same fate as Harris when he had to take his team into

Rentschler Field in 2006, falling to a game-winning performance by quarterback D.J. Hernandez, a player whose career at quarterback was so outstanding that when UConn came to Heinz Field a year later, he was playing wide receiver.

The game on September 23, 2007, was doomed from the start for the home team. Pitt took the ball in disarray at the beginning of the game. McCoy, having rushed for 172 yards a week earlier at Michigan State, wasn't even on the field for the Panthers' first offensive snap; that play was a handoff to fullback Conredge Collins for two yards.

On second down, quarterback Kevan Smith was sacked to lose seven yards. And before Pitt could run a play on third down, the play clock almost hit zero and Wannstedt had to call a timeout. Things seemed to be falling apart from the very beginning and they were about to get worse.

Once the offense had regrouped following the timeout, Smith dropped back to pass on third-and-15 and threw for tight end Darrell Strong in the middle of the field. But Smith never saw Danny Lansanah, and the UConn linebacker jumped the route for an interception that he returned to the 7-yard line. Three plays later and with only 1:49 off the clock, Connecticut had a 7-0 lead.

And somehow, things went downhill from there. Pitt proceeded to fall behind by 20 points before the first half was over, and the Panthers' drive chart looked almost as bad as the on-field product did:

Interception, punt, punt, punt, touchdown, punt, fumble. That last fumble came with less than 30 seconds on the clock in the second quarter; Smith had tried to scramble but lost the ball while getting sacked. UConn recovered and kicked a 39-yard field goal to take a 27-7 lead into the locker room at halftime.

The only positive Pitt really showed in the first half came, not surprisingly, from McCoy. The freshman running back was almost solely responsible for the Panthers' lone touchdown, throwing an 18-yard pass from the Wildcat before gaining 44 yards on three rushing attempts to reach the end zone.

But the coaches felt like they couldn't rely on the running game when the score was so strongly in the opponent's favor, so McCoy finished the game with just 11 carries for 70 yards and a touchdown. Rather than run the ball with their most talented player, Wannstedt and offensive coordinator Matt Cavanaugh felt like their best chance of coming back against UConn was to throw the ball.

That did not work.

The fans got excited, at least for a few moments, when Pat Bostick came out with the offense for Pitt's first drive of the third quarter. Finally, the Pitt faithful, believed, Wannstedt had benched Smith in favor of the freshman. But when the Panthers' first two drives with Bostick at quarterback each resulted in punts after three plays, the enthusiasm for Bostick turned into something similar to what Smith had experienced in the first half:

Boos.

On Pitt's third drive of the half, the Panthers finally converted a third down, which was, in itself, a rather significant accomplishment, since they had not achieved that objective since the Grambling game two weeks earlier. That success was short-lived, though; Pitt punted four plays after that third-down conversion, and on the Panthers' next drive, a Bostick pass was tipped at the line of scrimmage and intercepted by UConn linebacker Lawrence Wilson, who returned it 49 yards for another touchdown.

And on Pitt's next drive, Bostick did it again, throwing a pass right into the belly of UConn defensive end Lindsey Witten. That turnover didn't lead to a touchdown, but it didn't really matter at that point in the game. Nor did the 21-yard touchdown pass Bostick threw to receiver Oderick Turner the next time Pitt got the ball back. Even with that score, the Panthers were still down 34-14, and while they recovered an onside kick after the touchdown and drove close to midfield, another turnover - this time a fumble by McCoy on a pass from Bostick - killed Pitt's chances in totality.

Losing a close game to Michigan State on the road was one thing; Pitt's coaches, players and fans could stomach that. The Spartans looked like a good team and the Panthers had fought valiantly. But against Connecticut, a team that had won just one road Big East game in its history as a member of the conference, Pitt looked terrible. The defense played well enough, given the position the offense put it in with six total turnovers. But it would have taken a near-perfect defensive effort to win a game like the one against UConn in 2007. The defense would have had to not only hold the Huskies scoreless but possibly score a touchdown or two of its own to ensure victory.

Perhaps most troubling of all was the creeping fear that Bostick might not be a better option than Smith. Granted, the freshman quarterback's snaps against UConn represented the first significant playing time of his career, but he was not good in those snaps. Bostick attempted an exorbitant 41 passes in the second half of the game, completing 27 for 230 yards, one touchdown and three interceptions.

Those weren't the numbers people were hoping for when they clamored for Bostick to get the starting job. As long as he was on the bench and Smith was struggling on the field, fans could believe that their four-star quarterback recruit truly was the next Dan Marino; once he got on the field and showed his own range of struggles, those beliefs became a bit strained.

Hope can be a powerful elixir for sports fans. On the sidelines, Bostick represented hope. On the field, he threw three interceptions in the second half against UConn, and some more of that hope slipped away.

"PITT HAS NOT BEEN COOPERATING"

Pat McAfee's second missed field goal in the first quarter of the West Virginia game kept the score tied at zero, but as the first quarter turned to the second quarter, not much seemed to shake Pitt's offense loose.

The defense, on the other hand, was as good as ever. After the Panthers punted to open the second quarter, defensive coordinator Paul Rhoads kept West Virginia's potent offense off-balance by deploying a version of a 4-4 alignment - four defensive linemen and four linebackers instead of the three linebackers Pitt used as its base defense.

The Panthers were in that alignment when WVU quarterback Pat White dropped back to pass on a first down in the second quarter, but the left-handed passer didn't see Pitt defensive end Joe Clermond beat the Mountaineers' right tackle. Clermond got to White's blind side, hit him and knocked the ball loose; defensive end Greg Romeus fell on it and gave possession back to Pitt's offense.

"Pitt has not been cooperating," ESPN play-by-play announcer Mike Patrick said on the broadcast of e game. The defense was in control of a game against an opponent who had very much dominated the Panthers in the previous two years. And in 2005 and

2006, the Panthers had some top-shelf players, future NFL'ers like Darrelle Revis and H.B. Blades and Clint Session.

"When I talk with Coach Rhoads, he said that defense was like the no-name defense," says Scott McKillop, who was the starting middle linebacker in 2007. "We didn't really have any big names on that defense. We just all played well. We all bought in. We did exactly what was expected of us. And that's the thing about coaching: potential gets you fired, but consistency sometimes will carry you a lot longer.

"We had a lot of guys on that team that just did what they were expected to do."

The stat sheet for Pitt's defense from that season is littered with players who weren't stars the previous year. Greg Romeus was a redshirt freshman defensive end; he was second on the team in sacks (4) and tackles for loss (11.5). Aaron Berry was a first-time starter at cornerback as a sophomore; he led the team in interceptions (2). Joe Clermond, who led Pitt in sacks with 10.5, was a returning starter and an All-Big East performer, but no other player on the 2007 roster who recorded more than one sack had been a starter the previous year.

And McKillop was the biggest breakout of all. He led the Panthers with a whopping 151 tackles, 98 of which were solo tackles. He also had nine tackles for loss, three sacks, one interception, two forced fumbles and two fumble recoveries.

Not bad for a player the coaches had tried to recruit over a few times.

McKillop came to Pitt in the recruiting class of 2004, a local product from Kiski Area High School who had been a standout wrestler and a pretty good football player in his high school career. In his first three years of college, he sat behind H.B. Blades, one of the most prolific tacklers in Pitt history and the entrenched leader of the Panthers' defense.

The coaches weren't sending Blades to the bench for anyone; certainly not for McKillop. And while he knew that Blades was a special talent, McKillop also had his moments of doubt about his decision to go to Pitt.

"I wavered," he says. "I'll be honest with you: I wavered transferring to [University of Pittsburgh-Johnstown] to wrestle. I wavered potentially transferring to West Virginia. When you don't play and all you've done your whole entire life is play and start – nobody wants to wait your turn."

When 2007 came around, Blades was gone to the NFL and Pitt needed a new starting middle linebacker. The coaches had a few options, and they looked closely at Greg Webster, a second-year player who had been part of Dave Wannstedt's first recruiting class. They didn't know if McKillop could be a full-time middle linebacker, due to doubts about his size and his speed and his ability to make plays.

"I was not sure," Wannstedt says. "Scott had some intangibles from an intelligence standpoint and an instinct standpoint, some things in a linebacker that you don't coach. I always thought you had a group of players who could run over bags fast and do drills fast, stuff that you can coach and they're good players. But then you've got the guys that can do those things okay, and I always thought Scott was okay at those things, but he had instincts and he had intelligence and he was tough.

"He was one of the best tacklers we had at Pitt. If he got ahold of you, you were going down. So he had a lot of those things that you don't get to see unless they're playing. They don't show up when you're running scout team."

McKillop did enough in training camp 2007 to earn his opportunity as the starting middle linebacker. He was pretty sure he could do the job, but there's something to be said for getting on the field and actually doing it. The first test was the season opener against Eastern Michigan.

"It clicked that I could play Division I football in the first game of the season," he says. "It was the first play of the game and they ran a crossing route, and they threw it to the receiver and I picked him up and had him up pretty high - it could have been potentially a big hit. I made the tackle and I was like, okay, there it is.

"I think I had double-digit tackles in that game and the next game of the season was Grambling. But when I really started to believe I could play was against Michigan State when I had 18 or 19 tackles."

"I knew I had a good player, but I didn't know how high the ceiling could be for him," Rhoads says. "H.B. was a mentor to him, as far as bringing him along as a collegiate linebacker. But there were a lot of things that Scott figured out on his own. Scott's one of the smartest players that I ever coached in terms of common sense and really understanding the position."

McKillop started the season strong, and by the time the finale at West Virginia came around, he was a bona fide tackling machine. And that was a good thing, because Pitt needed everything it could get from McKillop and his partners on the defense that night. Because while the defense was holding Pat White and the WVU offense in check, Pitt's offense was sputtering.

After Romeus' fumble recovery, Bostick misfired on a pair of passes in short order and Pitt punted; when the defense stepped up for another three-and-out, the offense came up short again. LeSean McCoy was fighting for everything he got, trying to carry the team on his back whether he was taking handoffs or catching screen passes. But even as the offense slowly crawled across midfield, the passing game killed the momentum.

On a third-and-9 from the West Virginia 35, Bostick scrambled out of a shotgun formation to try to find an open receiver. What he found, instead, was WVU defensive back Vaughn Rivers, who picked off the pass for Bostick's second interception of the game.

With less than eight minutes left in the first half, Bostick had two complete passes and the same number of interceptions. The Panthers' defense was playing championship football; the Panthers' offense, by contrast, was just struggling to even possess the football.

DOOMED FROM THE START

In retrospect, some decisions aren't even worth trying to justify.

"I don't know; we must have seen something," Dave Wannstedt says now, either consciously blocking out or willingly ignoring the decision he made to open Pitt's game at Virginia on September 29, 2007.

Scott McKillop has no such uncertainty. He remembers exactly how that game started.

"Onside kick the first play of the game, and it was disaster ever since."

In his postgame press conference, Wannstedt said he thought Pitt would have a chance to "steal a possession," believing onside-kick specialist Cody Sawhill would catch Virginia off-guard. The idea was this: rather than kicking the ball deep on the opening kickoff, Sawhill would bounce the ball off the turf. Virginia's players wouldn't be expecting such a kick and thus would be slow to react; ideally, that would give a Pitt player or two time to get to the ball and recover it.

The Panthers would then take possession at or near midfield, giving the moribund offense some valuable "free" yardage.

That was the plan, and it almost made sense. Wannstedt had announced earlier in the week that Pat Bostick would replace Kevan

Smith as the starting quarterback. Citing a need to get a "spark" in the offense, the coaches planned to give Bostick a full game to show what he could do. But Wannstedt wanted to help the situation a little more by getting good field position on the first drive.

Hence, the onside kick.

The problem was, kickoffs only become "live" - meaning, either team can recover the ball - after the kick has covered 10 yards. Inside 10 yards from the point of the kick, only the receiving team can touch the ball. So while Sawhill's onside attempt did, in fact, catch Virginia off-guard, the whole plan went in the pot when Pitt redshirt sophomore walk-on Michael Toerper touched the ball before it went 10 yards.

The shame of it is, Toerper actually would have had a chance to recover the onside kick if he had let the ball go 10 yards. The Cavaliers truly were caught by surprise, so the play would have worked. But Toerper's early touch drew a penalty and gave Virginia the ball at the Pitt 39. And, as McKillop said, "it was disaster."

Virginia needed four plays after the kickoff to reach the end zone for a one-touchdown lead in less than two minutes. And that was the opening of the floodgates. Bostick's first possession as the starting quarterback lasted three plays and gained nine yards, and Virginia turned the ensuing punt into a five-play touchdown drive.

When the Cavaliers kicked off next, Pitt returner Lowell Robinson fumbled and Virginia recovered at the Pitt 26-yard line. Six plays later, the home team had another touchdown. And when Pitt went three-and-out again, Virginia made it count with a long punt return that led to a four-play touchdown drive.

With one minute and 22 seconds left in the first quarter, Pitt was trailing 27-0. The Panthers had only run six plays for 13 yards to that point and they were already down by four touchdowns. When they finally gained a first down for the first time in the game near the end of the first quarter, it was quickly undone by back-to-back false start penalties on Pitt's offensive line. And those two penalties added to the other five flags thrown on Pitt in the first 15 minutes of the game.

Somehow, "disaster" doesn't seem to do justice to the carnage.

By comparison to the first quarter, the final 45 minutes of Pitt's loss at Virginia that day in September – not surprisingly, the Panthers failed to dig out of the 27-0 hole – were relatively quiet. The Cavaliers kicked a field goal to extend their lead to 30-0, while Pitt finally reached the end zone in the second quarter after Virginia made one of its few mistakes on the day. Cavaliers returner Vic Hall fumbled a punt and Pitt defensive end Tyler Tkach fell on the ball, giving the Panthers possession at the Virginia 22. LeSean McCoy capped the drive with a one-yard run.

At halftime, Bostick had attempted just three passes. He completed all three of them for 29 yards, but the issues were clear: Pitt's coaches had little faith – perhaps rightfully so – in the team's passing attack. And with no passing attack, a 23-point deficit is virtually impossible to dig out of.

As Virginia pulled away even further in the second half, Wannstedt and offensive coordinator Matt Cavanaugh decided to let Bostick throw quite a bit. The freshman attempted 28 passes in the second half and finished the game with 181 yards, a touchdown, and an interception on 18-of-31 passing.

Not exactly a stellar stat line for Bostick's first start, but the experience was good for him.

"I got a chance to go out there and get some reps," says Bostick. "It got to a point in the game where it was pretty clear we weren't going to win the game, but I got some reps where I could kind of just cut it loose and not play as – I don't want to say conservative – but not play as judicious; just kind of go out there and wing it and play. I think that was valuable for me.

"That was valuable but everything else in the game was pretty bad. We took a beating and went back to Pittsburgh trying to figure things out."

By the time the final whistle mercifully blew, Pitt was trailing Virginia 44-14 and heading back to Heinz Field with a 2-3 record, a three-game losing streak, and pretty considerable questions across the board. No matter, though; the Panthers had some time off coming up with an 11-day break before the next game. And things should be okay, because their next kickoff was the following Wednesday against Navy; that should be a boost toward better outcomes, right?

A KEY CHANGE

In the second quarter against West Virginia, Pitt's offense was struggling but the Mountaineers weren't faring much better. The usually-potent WVU offense had to wait longer than expected to break out. But that breakout was coming; everyone at Mountaineer Field was sure of it.

After Pat Bostick's second interception in his first seven pass attempts in Morgantown, WVU looked poised to finally reach the end zone. Pat White and Darius Reynaud connected on an 11-yard pass to pick up a first down; then White completed a nine-yard throw to Steve Slaton for another first down. The Mountaineers were in Pitt territory and seemed to have momentum on their side.

After WVU moved across the 50, Slaton took a first-down handoff four yards to set up second-and-6 at the Pitt 45. On that play, Rich Rodriguez, who was the Mountaineers' head coach but called the plays - after all, he engineered the offense - went with a designed run for White rather than WVU's standard option-based attack.

White took the snap and ran to his left, but Pitt's defensive line got a push on WVU's offensive line - chiefly defensive end Greg Romeus, who ran left tackle Ryan Stanchek backward. Stanchek and Romeus occupied the hole White had hoped to run through, and the quarterback bounced off his blocker's back. A left-handed quarterback, White was carrying the ball in that hand, and to keep from falling down when he ran into Stanchek, he put his right hand on the back of his center, Mike Dent.

As players from both teams collapsed into a heap, White's thumb got twisted on Dent's back, and he was clearly in pain before he hit the ground. White stayed down after the play, cradling his thumb.

Sometimes an injury to a key player would cause a hush to fall over the crowd, but that didn't happen at Mountaineer Field as team trainers attended to White; rather, most of the faithful in attendance uttered some version of what was caught by ESPN's microphones as the television broadcast went to a commercial break and a WVU fan let out an exasperated "Goddamnit!"

"I think, to our kids, we were playing so well that it didn't elevate us that much," says Paul Rhoads, Pitt's defensive coordinator, about White leaving the game on that play. "We were playing really well to the point where they scored with the other guy, not with Pat White.

"There will be a lot of West Virginia people that will go to their grave saying, 'If Pat White hadn't got hurt, we'd have won that football game.' No chance. No chance. They did some things better offensively with the other guy in the football game."

The "other guy" was Jarrett Brown, a redshirt sophomore who had played in six games in 2006 and nine games in 2007 before the finale. His biggest exposure had come earlier in the 2007 season when he replaced White in WVU's loss at South Florida. White got hurt in that game as well, and Brown came in to throw for 149 yards, a touchdown and two interceptions while also rushing 15 times for 61 yards.

At 6-foot-4 and 220 pounds, Brown was bigger than White; he had a stronger throwing arm, too, and he could run pretty well for a player his size. But White was the catalyst of Rodriguez's option offense, the element that had turned the Mountaineers into national championship contenders. He would finish No. 6 in the voting for the Heisman Trophy that year, and when he left the game, Pitt's confidence had to rise. It certainly did among the small group of Panther fans who made the trip to Morgantown and the many watching from home.

Pitt was playing well, and taking White out of the game was only going to help that cause.

Brown had other ideas. He took over the WVU offense for a third-and-6 play, but instead of being a drop-off from White, he scrambled for a 14-yard gain and a first down. Next he completed a pair of passes that moved the Mountaineers inside the Pitt 15-yard line. The Panthers seemed to bottle things up after that, stopping Slaton for a two-yard loss and then corralling Brown on back-to-back runs, holding him to just one yard to set up a fourth down.

Once again, Pitt's defense had stood tall and turned WVU away. Pat McAfee, who had already missed two field goal attempts, would have to try a third time.

Before that could happen, the momentum took a blow. Defensive linemen Chris McKillop (the brother of linebacker Scott McKillop) and John Malecki had combined to make a great play in stopping Brown for a one-yard gain on third-and-12 from the Pitt 13, but defensive tackle Tommie Duhart drew a personal foul when he shoved a West Virginia offensive lineman after the play.

The lineman seemed to embellish Duhart's shove bit, flopping to the ground despite a push that didn't seem quite that heavy-handed. It didn't matter to the officials, though; they threw the flag and charged Duhart with a penalty that cost Pitt six yards and a fresh set of downs.

From first-and-goal at the 6, Brown took the snap and ran into the end zone for the game's first points. With 1:43 left on the clock in the first half, someone had finally scored. West Virginia had done what everyone expected - score first - and now that the

Mountaineers had broken the seal on scoring in the game, the floodgates were expected to open.

And what's more, they had reached the end zone with their best player – White – on the sidelines, getting an ice pack taped to his thumb while the team chaplain knelt beside him in prayer.

Pitt knew it would have a tough time handling White, but if Brown was able to drive on the Panthers and WVU was able to score with White out of the game, then the long night that everyone expected for the visitors might be on the verge of coming to fruition.

SINKING SHIP

October 10, 2007, was a Wednesday night, and anyone in the country who was interested in college football that evening had one option:

Pitt against Navy, live from Heinz Field on a nationally-televised ESPN broadcast. Rece Davis, former Notre Dame coach Lou Holtz, and Pitt great Mark May were in the booth to call the game. And there were more legends at the game, like Pitt's Tony Dorsett and Curtis Martin and Navy's Roger Staubach.

In the stands were 30,103 fans, an officially-announced number that was probably a slight stretch on the reality of that evening. After all, Pitt was a 2-3 football team, losers of three consecutive games that just so happened to be against the Panthers' three toughest opponents yet (clear implication: Pitt couldn't beat a good team). And Pitt didn't just lose to Michigan State, Connecticut and Virginia; each loss seemed to be worse than the last, from the near-miss at Michigan State to the miserable quarterback play against Connecticut to the ill-fated onside kick at Virginia that was only one of the many problems facing the team that day.

The last time Pitt had played at Heinz Field, an announced crowd of 40,145 showed its displeasure in the 34-14 loss to UConn with a chorus of boos. When the Panthers came back to their home stadium 18 days later to host Navy, 10,000 of those people didn't even bother to show up.

The ones who did go to the game against Navy probably expected the worst, given the outcomes of the previous three games. But there also had to be at least a glimmer of hope. After all, this was Navy; the Midshipmen were 3-2 at that point with wins over Temple, Duke and Air Force. Rutgers and Ball State beat Navy in Weeks Two and Three, respectively, and if nothing else, Pitt had to at least consider itself a better team than Ball State (Rutgers was another question; the Scarlet Knights were ranked No. 15 when they beat Navy and Greg Schiano's program seemed to be headed in the right direction).

Pitt still had plenty of question marks, of course, but the Panthers could take down Navy at home, right? It seemed reasonable to expect that they would come out of the game with an even record at 3-3 and head into the rest of the Big East schedule with at least a little momentum from a win.

10 years later, the players and coaches who were on Pitt's sideline that night still have some pain in their voices when they talk about the game. Like Paul Rhoads, the defensive coordinator on Pitt's 2007 team.

"That was the one game I hoped you wouldn't ask about," he said in the summer of 2017.

Or Scott McKillop, Pitt's middle linebacker that year.

"Embarrassing," he said and then repeated, perhaps not for emphasis as much as the merit: it deserved to be said twice.

"Embarrassing."

In 2007, Navy was coached by Paul Johnson, who had been the offensive coordinator at Navy in 1995 and 1996. He left the Midshipmen to spend five years as the head coach at Georgia Southern and then returned to be Navy's head coach in 2002. Throughout his career, he coached and refined and taught a triple-option offensive attack that came to be feared in college football.

In Johnson's offense, the quarterback takes the snap and starts reading individual defensive players. Based on what the quarterback sees, he can do one of three things: he can give the ball to a fullback running straight toward the line of scrimmage (the "dive"); he can run parallel to the line of scrimmage and flip the ball to a trailing slot-back (the "pitch"); or he can carry the ball himself (the "keep").

Dive, pitch or keep - those are the three options in the triple-option offense. Johnson, like other coaches who use the triple-option, has added elements to the scheme over time including tosses, sweeps and even pass plays, but at its heart, the triple-option is just that: three options for the quarterback.

What makes the offense truly tough to defend is that it thrives on the smallest of mistakes. A good triple-option quarterback only needs one defensive player to slip up, whether that means reading the wrong key, running into the wrong lane or attempting to do someone else's job on the defense, and when that happens, a good triple-option quarterback will make the defense pay.

Defending the triple-option is all about assignments: players have to know their assignments and execute them, if not perfectly, then close to it. The task gets even more difficult when a defense is preparing to face a triple-option offense in the middle of a season, when there's only so much practice time, only so much time in the film room, only so many reps to get comfortable seeing the triple-option work and understanding how to stop it.

The triple-option offense has cost many a defensive coordinator a good night's sleep. Some coaches will take time out of training camp in August to dedicate practice periods to working on the triple-option, even if the defense won't face that system for weeks or months into the season. On paper, stopping the triple-option is relatively easy; executing the right defensive approach with precision, accuracy and sound assignments is another story.

So while Pitt's defense after five games in 2007 was showing positive signs, the unit was still young, and defensive inexperience is like catnip for the triple-option.

"The Navy game was distinct because it's a triple-option team," Rhoads says. "You're not playing your defensive package, you go into it with something that's proven to defend it and then hope your guys can play it fast and tackle well and understand the adjustments that Navy's going to make and the cut-blocks and all of that. And it didn't work. Something that had worked before didn't work in that particular game."

"No question," Wannstedt said when he was asked if inexperience was the biggest issue against Navy. "When you have two days to practice and you have young players and you're trying to correct mistakes from the week before but you almost have to say, forget about the bad things that we did, we have to face an offense that we haven't seen before. To this day, you see it happen every year. We were just young. We were a young football team."

Paul Johnson and his Navy offense feasted on Pitt's youth and inexperience on defense. On the Midshipmen's very first play, Johnson turned the tables; he knew how geared up Wannstedt and Rhoads would have the players, how hard they would have coached them to watch for the telltale signs of whether the quarterback would hand the ball off, pitch it, or keep it. Johnson knew just what Pitt was going to be looking for the first time Navy snapped the ball. He knew the Panthers were keyed in on trying to stop the triple-option runs.

So he had his quarterback throw it. And on the first play of Navy's first series, quarterback Kaipo-Noa Kaheaku-Enhada faked a handoff and dropped a 49-yard pass into the hands of OJ Washington. Kaheaku-Enhada ran for 17 yards out of the triple-option on the next play, and then he and running back Reggie Campbell split the final 11 yards between them for a touchdown.

Like that, it was off to the races – for both teams.

Pitt and Navy combined to score 76 points over the course of four quarters that night, with LeSean McCoy rolling and Pat Bostick playing his cleanest game, completing a high percentage and only throwing one interception.

But for all the success Pitt was having on offense, the Panthers' defense was struggling, unable to find an answer for the triple-option attack. The Midshipmen ran for 331 yards against Pitt, with Kaheaku-Enhada going for 122 yards, fullback Eric Kettani running for 72 and four total players scoring rushing touchdowns.

"All the hype of Tony Dorsett being there and a [Wednesday] night game and we just didn't answer the bell," McKillop says. "That was the first time anyone had really played against a triple-option. Maybe our game plan wasn't as effective as it could have been, but they made the plays that they needed to make and we didn't. We just didn't have the stops we needed to, and point blank, they beat the crap out of us."

When the clock hit zero at the end of the fourth quarter, the game was tied at 38-38. Pitt got possession to open the overtime period and nearly had to settle for a field goal, but Navy – always one of the nation's most disciplined teams – jumped offsides on fourth-and-3, giving Pitt five yards and a new first down. From there, McCoy, LaRod Stephens-Howling, and Bostick each logged a rushing attempt to reach the end zone, with Bostick's one-yard sneak getting the score.

Navy had an immediate answer by bringing out a passing play – one of just 12 that Kaheaku-Enhada attempted in the game – and connecting for a one-play touchdown drive to tie the score again.

College overtime rules dictated that Navy got the ball next for its second overtime attempt. This time, the Midshipmen went to the running game until facing a third-and-6 at the Pitt 9; on that snap, Kaheaku-Enhada dropped back to pass but was sacked by Pitt defensive tackle Ernest "Mick" Williams, a huge play that forced Navy to kick a field goal for a three-point lead.

Pitt opened its second overtime possession by throwing when Bostick hit receiver Marcel Pestano with a great throw for a 16-yard gain to move inside the 10. McCoy then ran twice to get to the Navy 2, but on third-and-goal from that spot, offensive coordinator Matt Cavanaugh had Bostick drop back and attempt a pass to tight end Nate Byham. The pass was incomplete, but even if it had been caught, the play would not have counted since there was an illegal motion penalty called against the Panthers.

Navy head coach Paul Johnson declined the penalty to force Pitt into a fourth-and-goal at the Navy 2. Rather than kick a field goal to tie the game and send it to a third overtime, Wannstedt kept the offense on the field, looking to end the evening with a game-winning touchdown.

The next play ended the evening alright.

For the fourth-and-goal play, with Pitt needing just two yards to beat Navy, Wannstedt and Cavanaugh opted to not hand the ball to McCoy or fullback Conredge Collins - collectively, those two players had rushed for 217 yards and four touchdowns on 41 carries at that point - instead calling a play that had Bostick dropping back to pass again. The intended target was tight end Darrell Strong in the corner of the end zone.

The inexplicable pass was broken up, falling incomplete to send Navy out of Heinz Field with a 48-45 win.

"Obviously we liked the matchup with Darrell out there, and certainly I could have thrown the ball better," Bostick says. "In hindsight and probably in foresight, you would like to give the ball to Shady at least once, if not two or three times.

"They were so heavy in the box that they were asking us to throw it out there. But there was merit to running the ball once or twice there. I just have to do a better job of putting the ball on target and giving Darrell a chance to make a play."

The play didn't get made, though, and Pitt's three-game losing streak sunk to four almost entirely the back of a decision that defied logic and reason. Having Bostick throw on both of the plays from Navy's 2-yard line was widely lampooned at the time, and the highly questionable decision left the Panthers at 2-4 on the season, reeling and looking like they might not be able to beat anyone. The next six games were all against Big East opponents, and with big questions all over the roster, Pitt's 2007 season - as well as Wannstedt's time as head coach of the Panthers - was circling the drain.

"We played very poor defense and didn't live up to our end of it," Rhoads says in retrospect. "But at the same time, we had a chance to win the game. That one was painful. It was painful because we played poor defense. It was painful because we had a chance to win and didn't get it accomplished."

In his postgame press conference, Wannstedt offered some type of justification for the dual decisions of attempting that fourth-and-goal and then having Bostick throw rather than hand the ball to McCoy. 10 years later, that particular play has slipped his mind.

"I really don't remember. I'm trying to think - did we have a running back hurt or something? I definitely must be having an amnesia moment because, number one, I definitely don't remember it, and number two, for me to do that - that's completely against anything I believe in. Everybody knows that.

"I can't believe that that was really me."

A GLIMMER OF HOPE

When West Virginia scored its first touchdown with less than two minutes to play in the first half, it felt like a death blow.

Pitt had run six offensive drives at that point and gained a total of 49 yards. The Panthers punted four times, and the two possessions when they actually gained a first down ended in interceptions. Pitt's offense had run just six plays on West Virginia's half of the field, and three of those came from a possession that started on that side of the 50 after WVU fumbled.

The Panthers simply couldn't move the ball, and their slim chances of staying in the game with WVU hung solely on the defense's ability to keep the Mountaineers in check. But with Jarrett Brown's six-yard touchdown run that capped a 74-yard drive, it looked like that part of the game plan was falling apart, too.

After the Brown touchdown, Pitt took possession with around 90 seconds left in the half. If Dave Wannstedt was trying to portray an image of resilience and never-give-up attitude on the sideline, Matt Cavanaugh's offensive play-calling, ostensibly at Wannstedt's direction, didn't reflect it.

Of course, a conservative approach probably made sense; Pitt had the ball at its own 28, and driving 72 yards - which would more than double the Panthers' total offensive output to that point - seemed virtually impossible. So there wasn't much surprise when Pat Bostick handed the ball to LeSean McCoy on first down and second down and again on the next first down after McCoy's first two runs gained 11 yards.

But when McCoy's third run picked up seven yards and pushed the ball close to midfield, Wannstedt decided it was worth taking a shot at getting points and called a timeout to stop the clock. More than a minute had passed on the drive by then, and there were just 26 seconds left in the second half.

With the ball at the Pitt 46, Bostick came out of the timeout throwing to receiver Oderick Turner, who caught the pass for an eight-yard gain into WVU territory. But the officials threw a flag on the play, calling a late hit on West Virginia defender Reed Williams in a questionable call – broadcaster Mike Patrick called it "absolutely pitiful" – that nonetheless gave the Panthers another 15 yards.

All of a sudden, Pitt had the ball at the West Virginia 31-yard line with 17 seconds to go. Points, once thought to be a distant and unattainable dream, were now a starkly real possibility. Bostick knew the most important thing for him to do was to not throw a third interception, not in that situation, so when he dropped back out of the shotgun formation and saw nothing to his liking, he quickly threw the ball away.

With seven seconds left in the half, Wannstedt sent kicker Conor Lee onto the field to attempt a 48-yard field goal. Lee, a redshirt junior who was in his second season as Pitt's starting kicker, hadn't attempted a kick longer than 42 yards that season, and he missed both of his attempts from that distance. In 2006, Lee had made kicks of 46 and 47 yards, so 48 would be his career long if he could make it.

And he drilled it.

From the left hash mark, the native of Upper St. Clair, a suburb in the south hills of Pittsburgh, put the ball straight through the uprights as the clock hit zero. Despite recording just 75 yards of offense, despite gaining just five first downs, despite turning the ball over twice and not getting closer than 31 yards from West Virginia's end zone - despite all of that, Pitt ran into the locker room at halftime trailing their rival by four points. And the players did run; the surprise of points just before the first half ended sent a bolt of energy through the team.

The 100th playing of the Backyard Brawl was supposed to be another blowout for West Virginia, a game the Mountaineers would win walking away, embarrassing their neighbors to the north for the third year in a row as they set their sights on the national championship game in New Orleans.

At halftime, though, WVU had the lead but Pitt had the momentum.

"I thought there was something empowering for us knowing that we had nothing to lose that week," Bostick says.

A POP

In addition to the variety of issues facing Pitt in 2007, the Panthers also had a health problem or two.

Or six, because that's how many players who were expected to be contributors suffered season-ending injuries.

It started in training camp, when receiver Derek Kinder (knee), defensive end Doug Fulmer (knee) and running back Kevin Collier (wrist) were lost for the season. Then quarterback Bill Stull (thumb) was lost in the season opener against Eastern Michigan. Defensive tackle Gus Mustakas (knee) went down the next week against Grambling. And offensive lineman Jason Pinkston (shoulder) suffered a season-ending injury in Week Three at Michigan State.

But the injuries weren't limited to the players, though. After the Wednesday night loss to Navy, Pitt had 10 days before hosting Cincinnati at Heinz Field, a game that would turn out to be memorable for a few reasons, including one big reason for head coach Dave Wannstedt.

"You know why I remember that? I was on crutches," Wannstedt says. "I had just ruptured my Achilles tendon."

Wannstedt's recollection of the night he injured his Achilles is a classic example of Wannstedt-ian storytelling: It's probably based mostly in truth and it might have a few points where the truth is stretched, but either way, it's a great story.

"There was a group of us that played together and we would get together every week in the office at 6 o'clock and we would have a men's Bible group. There was probably six of us and we would get together for an hour and have coffee. We were all buddies from college.

"My Achilles had been bothering me since training camp and I was hustling down the hall and I remember Paul (Rhoads) was in there watching tape and I was walking by. He yelled, 'Hey Coach, you got a second?' and I stopped real quick. And when I stopped to turn, my Achilles popped. I literally fell to the ground, coffee went all over the wall and Paul was thinking I was having a heart attack. He's yelling down the hall "Hey guys! Hey guys!'

"Dave Blandino played with me at Pitt and he's a doctor, and he comes down the hall and as he's coming to me, he says, 'Don't tell me I have to give you mouth-to-mouth.' Paul thought I was having a heart attack. Dave thought I was having a heart attack. But my Achilles was rolling up in my leg."

By Wannstedt's retelling of the story, he called an emergency meeting of the coaching staff that night, had the team trainers prop his leg up on a table, and went over the practice schedule for the week. Then he went to the hospital to have surgery to repair his Achilles tendon.

And so a season that had already seen quite a few unbelievable twists took an even weirder turn. Now, Pitt was not just a 2-4 football team in a four-game losing streak, but a 2-4 football team in a four-game losing streak with a head coach who needed crutches. And when he didn't use the crutches, Wannstedt either drove around the practice field in a golf cart or motored through the halls of Pitt's football offices in a riding scooter.

"Dave was going around the facility in his scooter," quarterback Pat Bostick says. "We had forewarning when he was coming because you could hear him coming up the hallway.

"That's how I found out he had gotten hurt: I walked into the facility and saw him in the scooter. It was like when you were in the grocery store and turn a corner and there's someone on a motorized cart. That's kind of what it was."

That's how Pitt went into the matchup with Cincinnati, the Panthers' seventh game of the season. The Bearcats were ranked No. 23 in the nation with first-year head coach Brian Kelly, holding a 6-1 record after losing the previous week against Louisville, and they arrived at Heinz Field as the favorites against the 2-4 Panthers.

On Cincinnati's first drive, the Bearcats looked like the favorites. Ben Mauk was a graduate transfer from Wake Forest playing quarterback for Cincinnati, and he broke a 56-yard run the first time he touched the ball; six plays later, the Bearcats had a 7-0 lead, and they added a field goal on their next drive to go up 10-0 in the first quarter. Things were going according to expectations, and the home crowd was getting what it thought it would get from the team that had lost in double overtime to Navy 10 days earlier.

Except, Pitt started to show signs of life. Running back LaRod Stephens-Howling opened a drive with a 14-yard run and then took three direct snaps out of the Wildcat formation to pick up a few more first downs for the Panthers. In between, Bostick showed some surprising mobility to keep a play alive and connect with receiver Oderick Turner for 18 yards.

The drive stalled when Bostick and Turner couldn't connect on a third-and-3 play from the Cincinnati 24, but kicker Conor Lee was good on a 41-yard field goal to cut the lead to 10-3.

Two drives later, Stephens-Howling and freshman running back LeSean McCoy combined to run for 44 yards before tight end Darrell Strong jumped over a defender to catch a pass from Bostick in the end zone. Out of the blue, Pitt had tied the score with Cincinnati, and the Panthers had momentum in a game for the first time since the Week Two win over Grambling.

Cincinnati answered right back with a touchdown of its own and the Bearcats went into halftime up 17-10. But Brian Kelly wasn't happy, saying in his halftime interview that the first half was "embarrassing to watch," and while he is known for his over-the-top behavior on the sidelines, Kelly wasn't far off in his assessment. Through two quarters, Pitt had either played with or outplayed Cincinnati.

Still, the Bearcats had reasons for optimism. They had been an excellent team in the third quarter of games that year, holding a scoring advantage of +65 points in the third quarter through their first seven games. So while the 17-10 halftime lead wasn't as big as Kelly wanted it to be, surely Cincinnati would pull away in the third quarter; even when Pitt opened the second half with a field goal, the Bearcats were still likely to pull away.

After the way the Navy game went, it's likely no one expected what came next: Pitt's defense took control of the game. Cincinnati punted on both of its possessions in the third quarter, and after Mauk completed a pass to receiver Dominick Goodman early in the fourth quarter, Pitt cornerback Kennard Cox wrapped him up and defensive tackle Tommie Duhart came in for a big hit that knocked the ball out for a fumble. Safety Eric Thatcher and defensive end Chris McKillop dove on the ball to give possession back to the Panthers' offense.

Bostick and company didn't go anywhere with the turnover, but Lee came out for another field goal to cut Cincinnati's lead to one point at 17-16.

Pitt was trailing on the scoreboard but had all the momentum, and Cincinnati's next drive after the Panthers' field goal kept that momentum squarely in favor of the home team. On a first down from the Bearcats' 37-yard line, Mauk completed a 24-yard pass to receiver Butler Benton, but as Benton was dodging a tackle from Thatcher, linebacker Shane Murray stripped the ball from behind and Cox recovered it.

This time, the offense capitalized on the turnover and Stephens-Howling led the charge. He caught a 10-yard screen pass on the first play, ran for seven yards on the next play, and went on to account for 53 of Pitt's 61 yards on the drive – including a seven-yard run into the end zone to give the Panthers the lead.

The touchdown and ensuing two-point conversion fired up the crowd and the team alike. And when Pitt cornerback Aaron Berry intercepted a Mauk pass on the next drive – the Panthers' third forced turnover on the second half – the intensity grew. Pitt's offense needed to stay on the field for another two minutes and 48 seconds to run out the clock and secure the win. Cincinnati had two timeouts left so the Bearcats could still stop the clock two more times, and that meant the Panthers would need at least one first down and probably two.

On the first play, McCoy ran for two yards and Kelly called a timeout, stopping the clock at 2:43. On second down, McCoy ran for four yards and Kelly called another timeout. Facing third-and-3 with 2:37 left in the game, Bostick handed to McCoy again, and this time the freshman running back stepped through a hole on the right side of the line and ran for eight yards. First down.

The sideline erupted. The fans at Heinz Field did, too. A couple more McCoy runs picked up another first down and Pitt brought out the victory formation, taking a knee twice to end the game and give Wannstedt his first win against a ranked team as Pitt's head coach.

"We are told not to read the media; obviously, every person reads the media," says linebacker Scott McKillop, who had 16 tackles in the game. "I love it when coaches say, 'My players or I don't read it;' we all read it. And we all knew how much that game was going to mean to Coach Wannstedt. We knew that they had some players but so did we, and it just goes to show how close we were in so many games.

"Things like that are program-building wins. It was a huge win."

Central to the win was the two-headed monster of McCoy and Stephens-Howling. McCoy ran for 137 yards on 25 carries and Stephens-Howling had 100 yards and a touchdown on 13 attempts, the first time two Pitt players gained 100 yards in the same game since 1988, when Curvin Richards ran for 202 and Darnell Dickerson gained 108 in a 20-10 win over Rutgers.

For Stephens-Howling, it was his first 100-yard game since rushing for 154 in a loss at Connecticut the previous season. He hadn't run for more than 67 yards in the first six games of the 2007 schedule, and his high-water mark was a 67-yard performance in the season opener; after that, he only had one game with more than 16 rushing yards.

Stephens-Howling's limited production was largely due to his limited opportunities; that's what tends to happen to a veteran incumbent when a future NFL player joins the roster. The coaches and players knew right away that LeSean McCoy was a generational talent, the type of player who can change a team's fortunes from the time he walks on campus, and that was true: Pitt's records in 2007 and 2008 might have been markedly different if McCoy wasn't a Panther.

Everyone could see that "Shady" McCoy was the stud on the team, and that meant the other running backs had to move down a spot on the depth chart. Stephens-Howling, who had been a contributor and a starter since he was a freshman in 2005, suddenly found himself as the backup.

"It was obvious in practice," says Wannstedt, "as fast as LaRod was and as tough - I mean, LaRod was as tough as any of them; he was as tough as Shady and every bit as fast or faster than Shady -

but LeSean was 6'2" 210 and could break a few more tackles and stuff. LaRod was the guy that had gone through it from a freshman and had taken the licks and now another player comes in from a prep school, and I'll tell you what: there couldn't have been a better mentor and I think LeSean would be the first one to say that.

"When we started playing LeSean more, LaRod was his biggest fan. LaRod was a guy I used as an example all the time for the next three years in team meetings. If you ask any of those players, it was LaRod Stephens: here's a guy that's going to graduate, here's a guy that does everything right and he comes in here and he's an unselfish player. Everybody talks about those types of guys, and he's a real guy."

The coaches weren't the only ones who noticed how Stephens-Howling took his new role, and that made his 100-yard game in the huge win over Cincinnati that much sweeter for the whole team.

"LaRod did so much," says Bostick. "When Shady came, he could have easily pitched it in and not sat behind him and left or whatever, but he played special teams, he returned kicks, he'd block, he'd catch the ball; he made himself every bit as valuable as the backup as he was when he was the starting running back.

"We were fortunate to have him because he was a complement to LeSean. The one thing LaRod probably did for LeSean was, David Walker was our running backs coach and he was very good, but LaRod was able to provide some proof to LeSean that it's worth listening to Coach. Because LeSean would just as soon take a play that shouldn't go back-side and go back-side on it and make somebody miss; it looks great, but against a better opponent, it will get you beat. So LaRod was an influence on LeSean.

"You can't say enough about him. He was a great teammate and he made everyone around him better."

GOT IT

Momentum is one of those classic sports concepts that no one can really define, no one can really quantify, and no one can really predict, but everyone knows it when they see it.

And if anyone was doubting that Pitt had momentum coming out of halftime at West Virginia, what with the Panthers trailing the extraordinarily prolific Mountaineers 7-3, those doubts were erased about nine seconds into the third quarter.

West Virginia had won the coin toss at the start of the game and opted to defer its decision on receiving the ball until the second half, so Pitt was kicking off at the beginning of the third quarter. Pitt's punter, a left-footed Purdue transfer who dabbled in mixed martial arts named Dave Brytus, served as the kickoff specialist, and his kick at the start of the second half went to the WVU 13.

WVU cornerback Vaughn Rivers, who had attended Perry Traditional Academy in Pittsburgh, fielded the kick and followed his blockers to the 30, where he found a hole and flew through it, heading toward the sideline with enough daylight to make him - as well as the West Virginia fans - think he could have a chance for a really big return.

As Rivers crossed the 40, though, Pitt's Lowell Robinson zeroed in on him. Robinson had been one of the first Pitt players down the field, actually overrunning his position and seeming to get blocked out of the play. But the junior college transfer, who had played cornerback and wide receiver for Pitt but mostly served on special teams, turned on the jets.

Before Rivers could reach the 45, Robinson had caught up, and he knew exactly what he wanted to do. By the time Robinson was within five yards of Rivers, he already had his left arm in the air, ready to swing down on Rivers' left arm where he was carrying the ball.

Robinson caught Rivers at the 44, slapped the ball out and tackled him, and as Robinson and Rivers slid across the 45 toward the 50, Pitt cornerback Jovani Chappel fell on the ball right in front of the Pitt sideline.

And that sideline went nuts. Special teams coordinator Charlie Partridge, who was inches from the play when it happened, was signaling possession for Pitt before the referee did. Defensive coordinator Paul Rhoads, already known for his enthusiastic jumping after big plays, bounded his way into the scene. Head coach Dave Wannstedt, supported by a pair of crutches, limped toward the celebration as fast as he could.

On the West Virginia sideline, a stoic Pat White, his injured thumb in the pocket of a heavy coat on a cold Morgantown night, looked on without expression.

Pitt took the ball at the WVU 48, and while the momentum was with the Panthers, that was still a long way to go to reach the end zone. After all, Pitt's offense had generated just 75 yards in the first half; could the Panthers go 48?

Predictably, Pitt turned to LeSean McCoy to carry the load, and he ran for seven yards on the first two plays. Quarterback Pat Bostick threw to receiver TJ Porter on the third-and-3 that followed, but Porter was tackled for a two-yard gain, just shy of the lead sticks.

Facing fourth-and-1 from the WVU 39, Wannstedt, as conservative as ever, grudgingly sent the punt team out. And it clearly was a grudging decision; ESPN's cameras caught Wannstedt in a state of consternation on the sidelines, throwing his hands up in the air with a full display of disgruntled frustration – facial expressions that Pitt fans had come to know well.

For the Pitt fans watching at home, a fourth-and-1 at the WVU 39 meant an obvious call: go for it and try to make the first down. Line up, hand the ball to McCoy, and keep the drive alive. But they knew Wannstedt. They had watched Pitt's head coach make conservative call after conservative call in his three years leading the Panthers (and his 11 years as head coach of the Chicago Bears and the Miami Dolphins).

They had seen that look on the sidelines before, and here they were, seeing it again in a big moment against their hated rivals. But right after they saw Wannstedt's expression of frustration, they might have noticed something else.

They might have noticed Wannstedt muttering a quick aside to Bostick as he was coming off the field after the third down play.

"We're faking."

On Pitt's punt formation, linebacker Shane Murray lined up as a personal protector, standing midway between the long-snapper and the punter. Just before the snap, Murray, a quarterback in high school, ran up behind the center, took the snap, and pushed forward for a first down.

In the biggest game of the season and with momentum hanging in the balance, Wannstedt had gone for it. He called a fake punt and it worked.

"We worked on those every week, and here it was, the last game of the season," says Wannstedt. "You can't call them, you can't script them because it's got to be a certain area, it's got to be a certain down-and-distance, the score's got to be a certain thing one way or the other – there have to be about six things perfectly right before I would call it.

"Well, don't you know, we get a fourth-and-2 and everything was perfect; we called it and we got it."

With a fresh set of downs, the drive continued. Bostick and receiver Oderick Turner connected for an 18-yard pass on third-and-9 from the 35 to move inside the West Virginia 20-yard line. Fullback Conredge Collins took a handoff five yards to the WVU 12; then McCoy ran for eight to get inside the 5 and then three to get to the 1.

And on second-and-goal from the WVU 1, with Pitt's offense on the doorstep of the unthinkable - a touchdown - Bostick, who by his own admission was not very athletic, got his number called.

"We called 'Snoopy,' which was the quarterback sneak," he says. "Their defense was pretty condensed. I had Conredge behind me, but I knew I was going to have to give my best effort to even budge and get close to the goal line."

Bostick gave his best effort and then some. When the ball was snapped, right guard Joe Thomas pushed to his left, opening a hole on the right side of the line. Bostick knew he was going to take a hit, so he shuffled into that hole and turned his body to the left, putting his right shoulder forward and almost sliding sideways toward the goal line.

The hole gave Bostick room to run, but it also opened a wide space for West Virginia's defenders to tee off on the freshman quarterback.

And tee off, they most certainly did.

"I completely saw stars and blacked out for a second or five," says Bostick. "Typically, on a quarterback sneak, it's difficult to have a big collision because you're so close. But I took a pretty good shot on this one; it was almost as if someone wound up. Pat Lazear, the linebacker, he smacked me pretty good and punched me under the chin, too.

"I had gotten hit, turned sideways, bent over and Conredge was pushing my legs into the end zone. I landed on all fours with the ball over the goal line. It's hard to remember that because it happened so fast, but when you watch the tape, I don't know if there's ever been a quarterback sneak like that before and I don't know if there will ever be one like that again. It was as un-athletic of a touchdown as you'll ever see."

Call it un-athletic or whatever you like. It was a touchdown, and the crowd of 60,100 was loud in its silent observance of an unexpected fact: Pitt was winning. With 10 minutes to play in the third quarter, Pitt led No. 2 West Virginia 10-7.

36 INCHES SHORT

Pitt had its fair share of rough games in Dave Wannstedt's first two seasons as head coach of the Panthers; after all, he was 11-12 overall and 6-8 in Big East games. But of those 12 overall losses and those eight conference defeats, probably no two teams terrorized Pitt more in the 2005 and 2006 seasons than West Virginia and Louisville.

Led by two of the brightest offensive minds in college football, WVU and Louisville had poured it on against Pitt in Wannstedt's first two seasons. Neither team scored less than 42 points in beating the Panthers in 2005 or 2006, and the Cardinals and Mountaineers combined to record more than 2,000 yards of total offense in those games.

On average, Louisville and West Virginia had scored 45 points per game and gained 524.8 yards per game against Pitt with Wannstedt as the head coach. It was a debacle every time the Panthers tried to slow down either of those teams.

In 2007, Pitt traveled to Louisville to face the Cardinals the week after the Panthers upset then-No. 23 Cincinnati at Heinz Field. The Panthers had some good vibes at that point. The win over the Bearcats was Wannstedt's first victory against a ranked opponent and the team had gotten contributions from the whole team to win it. The running game with LeSean McCoy and LaRod Stephens-Howling was looking very strong. The defense was coming into its own. Even freshman quarterback Pat Bostick had played an efficient game and seemed to be maturing.

Plus, Louisville in 2007 was not what it had been the previous two years. While the Cardinals returned star quarterback Brian Brohm and 13 other starters from the team that had gone 12-1 and won the Orange Bowl in 2006, Louisville had lost two running backs to the NFL and, more importantly, its head coach.

Bobby Petrino was a masterful offensive guru, designing game plans and calling plays with such effectiveness that opposing defensive coordinators wondered how Petrino was so tuned into what they were doing. Never mind potential cheating; no one thought Petrino was listening to the opponent's headphone talk. He was so good that he seemed to be monitoring their inner thoughts, things they hadn't even said aloud.

After the 2006 season, Petrino left Louisville to be the head coach of the Atlanta Falcons. To replace him, Louisville hired Tulsa head coach Steve Kragthorpe. The Cardinals opened the 2007 season ranked No. 11 in the nation and climbed to No. 8 after beating Murray State in Week One. But things took a dive in Week Three when they lost to in-state rival Kentucky and again in Week Four when they lost to Syracuse.

By the time Louisville was hosting Pitt at Papa John's Stadium, the Cardinals were 4-4 - not much better than the Panthers' 3-4 record at that point.

Pitt didn't have the kind of coaching turnover that Louisville had experienced that offseason, but heading into the game against the Cardinals, the Panthers were in the midst of a semi-transition as well. Behind the scenes, the issues on offense had drawn quite a bit of Wannstedt's attention (and his Achilles injury cut into his focus as well). Something had to give, just in terms of the amount of time he spent with each unit on the team.

As a result, he pulled back a bit of his involvement with the defense, giving defensive coordinator Paul Rhoads some more autonomy at midseason.

"Well, I'd be wrong to say that wasn't a part of it," Rhoads says. "He was not as involved in everything as he had been prior to that. He spent some time up in the press box on game day because of immobility. Yeah, I think that probably did have an effect."

What that affected was how Rhoads designed and called the defense, starting with the Cincinnati game.

"I got back to being more aggressive," he says. "I probably got a little conservative, and I'm not going to necessarily say what influenced it, but I probably got a little conservative. And if you go back to Sunday's newspapers after the Cincinnati game, Brian Kelly was quoted as saying, 'I don't know what that team was or who that team is.' Because it was a personality and it was play-calling and game-planning different than he had seen that season going into that game."

Rhoads would need to be on top of his game for the contest at Louisville. While the Cardinals had a 4-4 record, they were still No. 5 nationally in total offense, averaging 529.8 yards per game. Brian Brohm was still one of the nation's top quarterbacks, having already thrown for nearly 3,000 yards after just eight games, and he got started quickly against Pitt, throwing touchdown passes on Louisville's second and third drives to jump out to a 14-0 lead early in the second quarter.

But Pitt's defense settled in after that. Defensive linemen John Malecki and Greg Romeus recorded sacks on one Louisville drive that really went downhill when the Cardinals took multiple penalties to end up in an unenviable second-and-42 situation. And on Louisville's fifth drive in the game, Brohm threw for receiver Harry Douglas, but Pitt cornerback Aaron Berry played the pass from behind Douglas, reaching around the future NFL receiver to bat the ball away before corralling it himself for an interception as he fell to the ground.

That pick happened on the first play of a drive for the Cardinals, and on the very next play, Pitt struck on offense. From the Louisville 27, Pitt quarterback Pat Bostick dropped back to pass and threw a lateral pass to tight end Darrell Strong. Strong was a quarterback in high school, and before Louisville's defense realized what was happening, he heaved a long pass to running back LeSean McCoy, who was standing all by himself on the other side of the field.

McCoy trotted into the end zone for an easy touchdown, and Pitt had cut Louisville's lead in half. But at halftime, the Panthers still trailed 14-7 and their offense was especially stagnant. Bostick had completed 3-of-8 passes for a grand total of six yards in the first half, while McCoy had 11 rushing attempts for 30 yards.

Louisville opened the second half with a field goal to extend the lead to 10 points, and that seemed like an insurmountable deficit for Pitt. Through the first three quarters, the Panthers had run one play on the Cardinals' side of the 50; that was the Strong pass to McCoy for a touchdown, which came after a turnover. They finally got into Louisville territory again in the fourth quarter and managed to get three points on a 35-yard field goal from Conor Lee, but they still trailed 17-10 with 10 minutes to play in the game.

Pitt's defense gave the ball back to the offense as the clock ticked under nine minutes. The Panthers were at their own 24, and while McCoy was, as always, the focal point, it was Bostick who stepped up and made some big plays. On third-and-5 from the 29, he threw to sophomore receiver TJ Porter, who picked up 10 yards on a crossing pattern.

Then, on third-and-10 from the 39, Bostick found fellow freshman Maurice Williams - who was playing more due to upperclassman Oderick Turner being slowed by injury - and

Williams made a great catch on a surprisingly good throw to pick up 15 yards. Two plays later, Bostick threw to McCoy on a wheel route up the left sideline, and the sensational running back made a terrific catch to pick up 30 yards and get the Panthers inside the Louisville 20.

From the 16, Bostick and Porter connected for a nine-yard pass, but junior running back LaRod Stephens-Howling lost a yard on the ensuing second-and-1. That brought up a third-and-2 from the 8; Bostick handed the ball to McCoy on that one, but he was stopped after picking up just one yard.

Now Wannstedt had a decision: kick a field goal to cut the lead to 17-13 with less than five minutes left? Or keep the offense on the field and try to keep pushing for a game-tying touchdown?

Wannstedt was upstairs in the booth that day; his Achilles surgery was still too fresh to risk having him on the sidelines. But he was in constant communication with Rhoads and offensive coordinator Matt Cavanaugh, who were down with the players, and he gave the call:

Go for it.

Pitt lined up for the fourth-and-1 at the 7 and, predictably, gave the ball to McCoy. He made it past the line of scrimmage pretty cleanly, and at the 5-yard line, he got hit from the front by Louisville players. Right around that time, he also got hit from behind by Pitt players, and the battle was on.

Players in both uniforms, positioned on opposite sides of McCoy, pushed with everything they had. Pitt's players pushed to get McCoy into the end zone. Louisville's players pushed to keep him out. Led by offensive lineman CJ Davis and tight end John Pelusi, the Panthers were victorious, willing McCoy over the final five yards to reach the goal line and a game-tying touchdown.

Pitt's sideline went nuts when McCoy scored. Now the defense, which had largely kept Brohm and Louisville's offense under wraps the entire game, had to get ball back to the offense one more time.

Unfortunately for the Panthers, two crucial mistakes cropped up on the next drive. First, a defensive holding penalty turned a potential third-and-10 into a first down. Then, a 25-yard pass from Brohm to fullback Scott Kuhn gained 27 yards - plus an extra few when linebacker Shane Murray grabbed Kuhn by the facemask. The pass and the penalty moved Louisville to the Pitt 7-yard line, and two carries by running back Brock Bolen the Cardinals into the end zone to take another touchdown lead.

With less than two minutes left in the game, Bostick, McCoy and Pitt's offense would need to drive 65 yards to try to get into the end zone and send the game to overtime. It was a tall order for the Panthers, but things went from bleak to promising when McCoy took a draw handoff from Bostick in the shotgun formation and ran for 19 yards on the first play. Then he did it again - same play, same 19-yard gain - on the next snap. And since the shotgun draw worked so well the first two times, offensive coordinator Matt Cavanaugh dialed it up again; this time McCoy picked up seven yards

After three plays and less than 20 seconds, McCoy had run for 45 yards and moved Pitt to the Louisville 20-yard line - all while running the same play three times in a row. On first down from that spot, Bostick threw his first pass of the drive, shooting for receiver Oderick Turner on a post pattern. Turner made a great catch and fell into the end zone, a brilliant finale to one of Pitt's best drives of the season.

But upon review, the referees ruled that Turner was down at the 1-yard line. Pitt's celebration of a game-tying touchdown would have to wait one more play.

Naturally, the Panthers turned to their bell cow from the 1, and Bostick took the snap and handed the ball to McCoy. But something went wrong. McCoy never secured the ball. It came loose. And Louisville cornerback Rod Council recovered it.

"It was a power play," Bostick says. "We had three tight ends and two running backs, so it was heavy personnel. The ball is supposed to hit inside.

"I think LeSean jumped a little bit when he saw some penetration inside, which is natural. But it's my job to make sure he gets it, because he's looking at the defense; he's not looking at the ball. I need to get him the ball between his upper arm and his lower arm and right between the 2 and the 5 (on McCoy's jersey). I hit him on the left oblique, I think, so it was a combination of him reacting, which is natural – trying to make a play – and me not doing a good enough job getting him the ball.

"We were both crushed after that game. We sat in a press conference afterward and I think we both took blame and we both meant it. I respected that a lot from him, because it's the quarterback's job to get him the ball. I needed to be the one taking the blame; not him. I really respected that from Shady."

Pitt's was 36 inches away from going to overtime with a chance for a quality win in an upset on the road. Louisville celebrated. Pitt was dejected. And no one was more dejected than McCoy.

"It's funny, the one thing I remember about that game is that's when I realized how much LeSean McCoy cared about Pitt," says linebacker Scott McKillop. "He fumbled the ball and he didn't shower, he didn't change his uniform; he rode home in his football pants. Not that I didn't know that he was a fantastic player, but that's when I knew that he cared. To see how much that bothered him..."

"F***ING PITT!"

Pitt fans will always point to Penn State as their chief rival in football. And given the option, they would likely pick Notre Dame as a second-most hated/favored opponent.

But the reality is, every Pitt football fan has a true, pure, and deep-seated hatred for West Virginia. And it's not just a simple hatred; it's one born of many elements, from proximity (just 70 miles separate Pittsburgh and Morgantown) to out-and-out condescension (Pittsburghers viewed themselves as metropolitan when compared to their neighbors across the state's southern border).

The hatred was intense on both sides of the rivalry. No matter where they were born, players who put on Pitt uniforms learned quickly that West Virginia was the team they disliked the most, and the same was true for those players who suited up as Mountaineers.

Pat Bostick, the freshman quarterback on Pitt's 2007 team, grew up in eastern Pennsylvania, where almost everyone was a Penn State fan, and those that didn't love the Nittany Lions pledged allegiance to Notre Dame. So he wasn't born into Pitt-West Virginia; he didn't know the history behind the 99 editions of the Backyard Brawl prior to that cold night in December.

Teammates and coaches and other people around Pitt had told Bostick what it would be like when the Panthers went to

Morgantown, but he didn't really get it until he was, as they say, in the belly of the beast.

"When you're driving into Morgantown and you see some lights finally - there's actually some society in West Virginia - you see some lights and all of a sudden you hear 'Bang! Bang! Crash!' and people are throwing full beer cans at your bus, you realize it's Pitt-West Virginia and it's for real. That's literally what it was.

"I was sleeping for most of the ride because I didn't feel very good. I woke up and saw the lights of the Coliseum and then - Bam! Whack! - it was like, 'What is this place and who are these people?' Then everything that everyone had told me about the rivalry began to make a lot more sense."

Bostick was on that trip because he was Pitt's starting quarterback, but it's not standard operating procedure for teams to take many freshmen beyond those who are contributing when playing on the road. Pitt coach Dave Wannstedt made an exception for that game.

"I took every freshman to the game. I put every one of those guys on a bus and everybody went to Morgantown. I didn't care. I wanted them to see what this was about and the importance of it. We had our entire football team on the sidelines for that game."

Before the game started, the freshmen weren't on the sidelines; they were with their teammates in the middle of the field, going through pre-game warmups in a fairly standard manner. Also standard is that both teams conduct those pre-game warmups at the same time; each has half the field, with the 50-yard line being the point where any contact will be made.

And on that night, contact was made.

"It's pretty much routine that, when you're doing 11-on-11 warmups, you kind of form a line behind your offense; that was the front lines," Bostick says. "I mean, there was more hooting and hollering there than I can remember in any game I ever played in.

And it was mainly us. Our guys were trying to instigate. We had nothing to lose."

That was in the pre-game. By the time Pitt had a three-point lead in the third quarter against West Virginia, the Panthers were rolling. They had stymied the Mountaineers' offense and then, against all odds, had scored a touchdown of their own. And it was a rushing touchdown by decidedly-immobile quarterback Pat Bostick, no less.

If West Virginia fans were stunned by Pitt scoring a touchdown, their own offense didn't do much to pull them out of their slumber. The Mountaineers went three-and-out and punted after the Panthers scored, and the crowd of 60,100 grew more and more restless.

Meanwhile, Pitt's defense kept playing better and better. WVU speedster Noel Devine was dropped for an eight-yard loss on the Mountaineers' first play after the Pitt touchdown. On second down, quarterback Jarrett Brown threw a screen pass that gained zero yards. And on third down, Brown nearly fumbled the ball when he essentially dropped it, but the game officials said that he was in a throwing motion and ruled it an incomplete pass.

Pitt would have liked to have the fumble, but an incomplete pass worked just fine, too. And when that ball hit the ground, the Panthers' sidelines got even rowdier, so much so that the referees issued a sideline warning on the visitors - essentially telling Pitt to calm down.

Defensive coordinator Paul Rhoads could be as animated as anyone, and the sideline warning was probably on him as much as anyone. But the veteran coach couldn't help it: his players were doing exactly what he wanted them to do.

"We understood the importance of tackling going into that game because, believe me now, we'd been shredded in the past by (Steve) Slaton and Pat White," Rhoads says. "They shredded us.

And our guys knew the importance of it. So we worked tackling hard and tackled awfully well.

"We only missed two tackles that night, and the extra yardage that West Virginia got after those two missed tackles was seven yards total. You're going to win a lot of football games when you play like that."

The players were doing it. They were executing the play calls well, and when they had a chance to tackle White (before he got injured) or Slaton or Devine or Brown, they made the plays. Linebacker Scott McKillop was leading the charge, and he was taking his cues from the coach calling the plays.

"Every single time we'd come to the sideline, Coach Rhoads would preach to us: Believe, believe, believe."

After Pitt's defense forced another West Virginia punt, the Panthers' offense took the field again looking to repeat the touchdown they scored the last time they had the ball. Naturally, freshman running back LeSean McCoy got the call early and ran to set up a third-and-3, at which point the coaches turned to junior LaRod Stephens-Howling, who caught a shovel pass to pick up a first down.

After West Virginia's nose guard jumped offsides on the next first down, McCoy broke his biggest run of the game, taking off for 19 yards to get inside the WVU 30-yard line (it's a testament to how hard McCoy ran in the game that his longest run was only 19 yards; the freshman back earned everything he got in Morgantown that night).

McCoy's long run caused even more uneasiness among the West Virginia fans, including one who was caught on ESPN's broadcast yelling out "F**king Pitt!" This wasn't supposed to be happening; their Mountaineers, heroes of the state, were supposed to be headed for the national championship game. Instead, they were in a dog fight with their hated rivals, a 4-7 team that had no business being within four touchdowns of West Virginia - let alone holding a lead well into the second half.

Pitt kept going, though. Using a combination of McCoy, Stephens-Howling, and fullback Conredge Collins (who converted a key fourth-and-1), the Panthers pounded their way to the 13 before McCoy made an unbelievable run to get into the end zone for Pitt's second touchdown in as many drives.

But the celebration quickly turned to outright anger, as the referees called a holding penalty on Pitt receiver Oderick Turner.

The penalty negated the touchdown, and Wannstedt was beside himself on the sideline, throwing his crutches and screaming at the official who threw the flag.

"That's a bullshit call!" Wannstedt yelled (his complaints were picked up on the ESPN broadcast). "How can you call that?!"

Upon further viewing, Turner had his left hand outside the jersey of a West Virginia defender for what looked to be, at best, a questionable call. Nevertheless, the penalty pushed Pitt back to a third-and-10 at the 17-yard line, and Bostick's pass to tight end Darrell Strong lost a yard.

Wannstedt sent kicker Conor Lee out to attempt a 35-yard kick, and while Lee had been good from 48 yards at the end of the first half, he missed this one, and the score stayed at 10-7 in Pitt's favor.

A NEW WAY TO LOSE

Emotions were raw around the Pitt football program after the loss at Louisville. The fumbled handoff between freshmen Pat Bostick and LeSean McCoy was a mistake, an accident born of youth but ultimately not the kind of thing that would, in a vacuum, break a team's spirit.

2007 was different, though. Pitt's spirit wasn't broken by the loss to the Cardinals, but the team's psyche definitely took a blow. Here they were, facing a team that had tormented them for two years running, and they had nearly pulled off a road upset. They had nearly overcome a wealth of obstacles and adversity and challenges to mount an inspiring win.

But they couldn't pull it off.

Instead, the momentum the Panthers built in their win over Cincinnati two weeks earlier was gone. Pitt was a 3-5 team with major issues at quarterback, a coach who couldn't walk, and a creeping sense of dread about the long and short term for the program.

Eight games into a 12-game schedule, 2007 was looking like a doomed season - and possibly more - for Pitt.

For the ninth game of the year, Pitt welcomed Syracuse to Heinz Field. The Orange were coached by Greg Robinson. Syracuse had hired him in 2005, and like Dave Wannstedt, who was also hired that year, Robinson had spent the bulk of his recent coaching career working in the NFL. The early results of Syracuse's decision to replace long-time coach Paul Pasqualoni made the early run of Wannstedt's tenure at Pitt look like a smashing success.

In Robinson's first year, Syracuse had won one game; the next year, the Orange won four (the NCAA has since vacated those five wins). Heading into the game against Pitt in 2007, Robinson had Syracuse at 2-6; the Orange were in a race with the Panthers to see which team could avoid being the clear worst in the Big East, and the reality of Pitt's possible position in the basement of the league had everyone on edge.

So when a reporter asked Wannstedt during the week leading up to the game if he was confident his players would not be overlooking the 2-6 Orange, he looked up from his golf cart and bristled at the suggestion.

"Are you kidding me? We've got three wins."

Wannstedt was right: Pitt had three wins at that point. But no matter how low Pitt's season would sink, the Panthers still weren't as bad as Syracuse. The game they played on the first Saturday of November at Heinz Field wasn't very good as far as games go, but the home team still managed to come out on top.

Syracuse struck first with a field goal, but Pitt answered in short order when Bostick and receiver Oderick Turner connected on a great throw-and-catch. Pitt kicker Conor Lee hit a field goal to end the half with Pitt leading 10-3, but a Syracuse touchdown was the only excitement in the third quarter, and it left the score tied heading into the final frame.

Fittingly, it was McCoy who broke the game open when he took a pitch from Bostick and ran into the end zone for a touchdown. Lee would add an insurance field goal after that, which came in handy when Syracuse scored one more touchdown late. But Pitt's defense made sure that the Orange didn't see the end zone again, and the game ended with the Panthers ahead 20-17.

Two storylines emerged from the Syracuse win, though, and both were reflective of larger narratives in the 2007 season. The first was McCoy, who ran 31 times for 140 yards and a touchdown and passed the 1,000-yard mark for rushing, making him the first Pitt freshman to rush for 1,000 yards since Curvin Richards did it in 1988.

The Syracuse game was the fourth 100-yard game in a row for McCoy, who put up 562 yards and five touchdowns in that stretch. In a season that was lacking for bright spots, McCoy provided more than a few.

"He was the most talented player I ever played with, but he was also the hardest worker in practice," says Bostick. "No one practiced harder than him."

The other bright spot in the Syracuse game and the season as a whole was the defense. Pitt held Syracuse to just 265 yards of total offense and only two third-down conversions on 14 attempts. The Orange didn't have a dominant offensive attack, but the defensive performance from the Panthers that day was becoming the norm. Pitt's young defensive line was coming into its own, the defensive backs were becoming more confident, and linebacker Scott McKillop was looking like one of the best players in the Big East.

With 12 tackles against Syracuse, McKillop topped the 100-tackle mark for the season, and he still had four games to play. The redshirt junior who hadn't been expected to win the starting middle linebacker job was playing far above what just about anyone thought he could do.

"Being the notable wrestler that he was, he was a great tackler because of that," says Paul Rhoads. "He was not an overwhelming physical tackler, but he was an unbelievable 'get-them-to-the-ground-finish-the-play' tackler. And he was a lot faster than people would realize. You know, he was big, he was heavy, he was in the 240-250 range, and white and didn't look like he was running fast. But Scott was a fast player."

Michigan State found out how fast McKillop was when he recorded 17 tackles in Pitt's loss in East Lansing in September of that season. The same goes for Virginia (15 tackles), Navy (14 tackles) and Cincinnati (16 tackles). Pitt's defense was turning into a formidable unit, and McKillop was leading the way.

"He's got such a great personality that he got along with most and they all knew what to expect from him," Rhoads says. "They all knew what he was going to give them, especially from a toughness standpoint and a resiliency standpoint. And I think, you know, when you get put in a leadership role with those qualities, people are quick to follow."

Two weeks after the defense effectively dominated Syracuse - Pitt had an off week following the Syracuse game - the Panthers went to Rutgers and the expectation was that the results would be similar, even though the Scarlet Knights were more talented than Syracuse.

Rutgers had a star running back in Ray Rice as well as NFL draft picks Tiquan Underwood, Courtney Greene, Jason McCourty, Devin McCourty, Mike Teel, Kenny Britt, Ryan D'Imperio, and Anthony Davis. The Scarlet Knights had even entered the 2007 season ranked No. 16 in both the Associated Press poll and USA Today Coaches Poll; it was the first time in program history that Rutgers was ranked in the preseason.

Rutgers held a curious position for Pitt and Dave Wannstedt. Greg Schiano was the coach of the Scarlet Knights, and he had been a defensive assistant for Wannstedt for three seasons when Wannstedt was the head coach of the Chicago Bears.

Familiarity had bred some contempt, but for the first two years of Wannstedt's time at Pitt, his former apprentice had the upper hand. Rutgers beat Pitt in 2005 and 2006, but even with an 0-2 record against Schiano, Wannstedt couldn't help but think his team still held a superior position over its Big East foes from New Jersey.

"In my mind, even though I knew and respected Greg and knew the kind of coach he was and knew the players they were getting there - he was doing a better job than anybody else had done - I still had the feeling, and it was a little bit of my problem at Pitt, too, I had the feeling that we should be better than them," Wannstedt says now. "I don't care who's coaching them or I don't care what players they have; we're Pitt and that's a game that we have to win."

But Pitt hadn't beaten Rutgers since 2004 - the year before Wannstedt arrived. When the Panthers got to Piscataway in November of 2007, the Scarlet Knights had fallen out of the national polls, sitting at 6-4 overall and 2-3 in the conference. Pitt wasn't in great shape at 4-5, but the Panthers' Big East record was the same as what Rutgers was working with, and that Saturday's game would give Wannstedt's team another chance to take a step forward.

If Pitt was going to beat Rutgers, the Panthers had to stop Rice, the Scarlet Knights' star running back. In the previous two games against Pitt, he had rushed for 339 yards on 54 carries - 6.3 yards per carry - and in the first 10 games of 2007, he had topped 100 yards seven times, including a 243-yard game the week before he faced the Panthers.

Rice was a stud, and Pitt knew it had to find a way to contain him, just like Rutgers knew it had to find a way to contain McCoy. And from the start of the game, it was clear that Wannstedt and Schiano were each focused on the other's star running back.

On the first play of the game, Rutgers went to Rice and McKillop followed, making a tackle for a two-yard gain.

"He was a grown man in college," McKillop says. "He was as big and thick in college as he was in the NFL. And they had a huge offensive line. Biggest one I ever played."

McKillop was more than up to the task. His tackle on Rice on the first play of the game was the first of 16 tackles he made that day, including 10 solo stops.

"It's funny, because if you ask a lot of Pitt fans and reporters, the one game they remember me for is the West Virginia game," McKillop says, "and truth be told, I didn't even really have the type of game that I could have had. I feel like one of my better games statistically was the Rutgers game. I was in a zone and I felt like I couldn't be blocked. No matter what they did, I dominated."

That's not hubris; McKillop truly did dominate. In addition to his 16 tackles, he had 2.5 tackles for loss, 1.5 sacks, an interception, three pass breakups, and a forced fumble. He made plays all over the field, but Rutgers still found ways to move the ball. Receiver Kenny Britt got behind Pitt cornerback Kennard Cox for a 53-yard touchdown pass in the first quarter, then Rice showcased his cut-back ability to break a 28-yard touchdown run that put Rutgers ahead 17-10 at halftime.

Pitt's lone touchdown in the first half came on a pass from Pat Bostick to tight end Darrell Strong, a well-placed fade throw that almost functioned like a basketball alley-oop. The problem was, that touchdown was one of just three passes that Bostick completed in the first half, and he went to the locker room with 35 yards on 3-of-10 passing plus three sacks as Rutgers took advantage of his lack of mobility.

That was Bostick's stat line when he went into the locker room; when he came out for the third quarter, he did so with the knowledge that Wannstedt was going to try Kevan Smith, the redshirt freshman who had started the Grambling, Michigan State, and Virginia games, at quarterback.

"I played awful in the first half," Bostick says. "I went into halftime and they let me know they were going to make the switch, and I was devastated. That hurt. As a freshman, you're already somewhat vulnerable and you're malleable - that's the hard thing about playing freshman quarterbacks: good or bad, you're going to affect them as they move forward in their development. It's a very formative time for them.

"I was pretty crushed and I don't think I paid a whole hell of a lot of attention at halftime and I was pretty pissed off. He let me know that I needed to keep my head in it and they were going to need me."

Smith, in his first playing time after sitting out the previous five games, gave Pitt a little hope on his first play when he took a snap in the shotgun and ran a quarterback draw for 15 yards. As the second half progressed, he led the Panthers to a pair of field goals, cutting Rutgers' lead to 17-16 in the fourth quarter.

The Scarlet Knights came back with a field goal of their own to push the lead to 20-16, but Smith, with some confidence behind him, led the offense onto the field looking for a go-ahead touchdown. After he scrambled for a first down on third-and-2, though, Smith came up in pain. He didn't leave the game, but it was clear that Smith was hurt, and when Rutgers sacked him on a third-and-13 play later in the drive, it was clear that he had injured his shoulder.

So when Pitt's defense forced Rutgers into a three-and-out and gave the ball back to the offense on the next possession, Wannstedt went back to his freshman quarterback.

Pat Bostick ran back onto the field with Pitt's offense starting a possession at the 40; there were just under three minutes left in the game and the Panthers needed a touchdown. The coaches turned to McCoy initially, as Bostick didn't throw a pass until the fourth play of the drive. But he completed that one - a five-yard pass to receiver TJ Porter - and then completed two more short passes to move the ball past midfield.

With less than 40 seconds on the clock and Pitt facing a third-and-7 from the Rutgers 34, Bostick floated a pass to Strong, and the big tight end broke a tackle to run for 28 yards before getting downed at the Rutgers 6. Pitt's offense rushed to the ball and Bostick spiked it to stop the clock with 25 seconds left.

With second-and-goal at the 6, the Panthers were set up for the win. This wasn't the same as the situation at Louisville three weeks earlier; in that game, Pitt needed a touchdown to tie the score and force overtime. At Rutgers, a touchdown would win the game. And on second-and-goal, Bostick threw a fade to Oderick Turner, who out-jumped Rutgers cornerback Jason McCourty to make the catch and stay inbounds for the game-winning touchdown.

Until a flag was thrown.

The official standing near the left side of the end zone, where Turner had caught the ball over McCourty, saw contact and made the call: offensive pass interference on Turner, negating the touchdown and pushing Pitt's offense back 15 yards.

The play gutted the Panthers.

"It was just an awful call," Bostick says.

"That just killed me because I really felt we should have won the game," says Wannstedt. "The players felt that way, the film looked that way and it just didn't happen.

"I was upset every week about calls with officials, but that may have been as upset as I was about a call. I had a long session with the Big East officiating crew Monday morning on the phone. It took me awhile to get over that call."

Pitt failed to reach the end zone on the subsequent plays, and the Panthers got on the plane back to Pittsburgh with a 20-16 loss to Rutgers that dropped them to 4-6 on the season. They had lost the other five games because of bad play calls, bad quarterback play, and bad luck; now they could add bad officiating to the list.

THE TELL

The loss at Rutgers took Pitt's season to new depths, but the Panthers didn't come home from New Jersey empty-handed.

"This is the game that actually laid the groundwork for the West Virginia victory," says Paul Rhoads.

Mike Teel was the quarterback for Rutgers, but the Scarlet Knights also had a different package they used. The package featured Jabu Lovelace, a backup quarterback whose biggest attribute was his speed; he attempted 23 passes in the 2007 season, but he ran the ball 81 times.

Essentially, Lovelace was running an option offense for Rutgers, and the week before the Pitt game, he had helped lead the Scarlet Knights to a 41-6 win over Army. Lovelace was a big part of that victory, rushing for 81 yards and two touchdowns. Rhoads and the Pitt defensive staff knew they would have to prepare for Lovelace and that package of special plays.

"We had to devise a plan for that and it was a pressure package that we put in for that personnel grouping, and we ran them out of it," Rhoads says. "That was the end of that package for them."

It sure was. Lovelace recorded 13 rushing attempts against Pitt and finished with a net total of one rushing yard. Pitt's pressure package had defeated Rutgers' quarterback-run package, and that got Rhoads to thinking:

If it could work against Rutgers' running quarterback, could it work against West Virginia's?

"The light went on for me that it was something we could probably use against them more extensively if it worked. And obviously it did and worked with great success. I thought through film study that West Virginia would see it and be expecting it, but I never got the feeling that they were prepared for what we were going to bring. Because other than the Rutgers game, we had never shown it against them in any shape or form before.

"That was the big piece of our game-plan against West Virginia in that final game. Maybe without that exposure in the Rutgers game, we never would have been in position to play that or stop West Virginia as soundly as we did."

Rhoads isn't inclined to give up trade secrets, but Pitt's approach focused on controlling how the quarterback would make decisions. Rich Rodriguez's offense is based on reads the quarterback makes after the ball is snapped; Rhoads wanted to make those decisions for White - and make them in Pitt's favor.

Based on what he learned from game-planning for Lovelace, Rhoads and the Pitt defense set out to force WVU quarterback Pat White to not do the things he wanted to do; rather, the Panthers wanted White to do what they wanted him to do. They wanted to make him keep the ball when they were set up to stop him from running it and they wanted to make him hand the ball off when they were set up stop the running back. And they believed they had the defensive strategy to do it.

The problem is, Rhoads was sure that Rodriguez would scout the film from the Rutgers game while preparing for Pitt, especially since the Scarlet Knights had a quarterback that roughly approximated what he tried to do with Pat White. Rhoads thought Rodriguez would see what Pitt had done against Lovelace and be prepared for it.

And he was surprised to find out that wasn't the case.

"Absolutely. Absolutely. Because what we did, it was all-out pressure. There was nobody in the middle of the field and it was man coverage and we were attacking their run game and counting on the quarterback to make reads based on what we were doing. We wanted to determine what their quarterback was going to do with the football. And as it played out, that's exactly what happened.

"There's a play in the second half of that game, a fourth-down stop, where they ran a play and the play played out exactly like we wanted it to, based on how we were defending it. They showed Coach 'RichRod' on the sideline and he's got his hands to the side like, 'Why didn't you keep that?' And we knew he wouldn't. Based on what we showed him, we knew he was going to give the ball and we had somebody right there to tackle the ball-carrier when that happened."

Pitt linebacker Scott McKillop said that the Panthers had seen something else in Lovelace that carried over to the West Virginia game.

"It was the foot of the quarterback," says McKillop. "When the quarterback's feet were parallel, it was a zone read. When one foot was in front of the other, he was passing. I think we were ahead of our time. Right now, you have 37 coaches on your staff looking for every little detail like that. But at the time, that was one of the things we saw on film and it was easy."

By the end of the third quarter, Pitt was making it look easy. Placekicker Conor Lee had missed a field goal from 36 yards, but the Panthers still led 10-7 and when West Virginia took the ball back at its own 20, the momentum was squarely with the visitors.

On the first play of that next drive, WVU quarterback Jarrett Brown was dropped with a big hit from Pitt's Jemeel Brady. One of the unsung heroes that night in Morgantown, Brady was a redshirt senior making his third career start and his first at linebacker, the position he moved to after spending the previous four years at safety.

Brady's hit jarred the ball loose, and the Mountaineers were fortunate to have fullback Owen Schmitt fall on the fumble. That play ended the third quarter, and for Pitt, the fourth quarter couldn't start soon enough.

"When the third quarter ended, our guys took off to the opposite end of the field," Rhoads recalls. "Somebody made a comment to me about that and I remember going back and watching that on the TV copy. That was just the kids. They were in control of the football game and they just wanted to keep playing."

When the break for the change in quarters ended, Pitt picked up where it left off. Brown was hit by McKillop for a one-yard loss on the first play of the fourth quarter, and on third-and-8, a well-timed blitz call by Rhoads forced Brown to overthrow his intended receiver, and WVU was punting again.

Pitt's lead was slim at that point – just three points – but the Panthers were in control, so much so that even when their offense had to punt, it seemed to be a win for the visitors. After WVU punted, Pitt took the ball with 14:06 left in the fourth quarter and two goals in mind: try to get some points and run the clock in an effort to keep WVU's offense off the field. And those goals didn't exactly take priority in that order.

To that end, Pitt accomplished at least part of what it set out to do. Quarterback Pat Bostick made a big play – one of his first in the game – with a 26-yard pass to tight end Darrell Strong to convert a third-and-10 and keep the clock ticking. And while the offense didn't go much further down the field after that, the Panthers had still taken more than three minutes off the clock, giving the ball back to WVU with 10:28 left.

By that point in the game, Pitt's defense probably couldn't wait to get back on the field. The punt by Dave Brytus had been downed at the WVU 3, forcing the Mountaineers to go a very long way if they wanted to get points. So even though WVU quarterback Jarrett Brown ran for 11 yards on the first play of the drive and threw for nine yards on the next snap, Pitt's defense knew it still had the upper hand. And on first down from the WVU 26, the Panthers came up with the biggest play of the game - which is saying something, given the number of big plays the defense made.

After picking up two first downs, Brown dropped back to pass from the 26, but defensive tackle Tommie Duhart, a junior-college transfer who worked in a reserve role for Pitt in 2007, blew between the right guard and the right tackle to get into the backfield. Brown saw Duhart and tried to throw the ball before Duhart got to him, but Duhart was too quick: he hit Brown just before he could make the pass. As Duhart dragged Brown to the ground, the ball came out, and Duhart crawled over Brown to fall on the fumble and recover it.

Pitt's third fumble recovery of the game was its biggest one yet, and it set up the offense at the WVU 17.

FINAL ADVERSITY

As Pitt got ready for its home finale against South Florida, the Panthers were low. The loss at Rutgers on a bad penalty had compounded the issues the team had experienced all season, and now they were 4-6 and facing a good South Florida team that was ranked No. 23 and had beaten them a year earlier.

In the Rutgers game, Dave Wannstedt had made the halftime decision to bench Pat Bostick and give Kevan Smith another chance; that seemed to be an effective change, as Smith played well until he injured his shoulder near the end of the fourth quarter. Smith's injury brought Bostick back into the game, and in the week between Rutgers and South Florida, it became clear that Smith's shoulder would not heal enough for him to play against the Bulls.

So Bostick was back as the starting quarterback. And while an early drive against USF looked doomed when he dropped the ball on a handoff attempt and lost six yards, the freshman quarterback recovered and connected with LeSean McCoy on a screen pass that gained 25 yards to convert a third-and-10 situation. Five plays later, McCoy took a toss to the right and ran into the end zone for a touchdown.

USF answered that touchdown near the end of the first quarter, but Pitt's next two drives didn't produce points, as the Panthers failed to convert fourth-down attempts on each possession (including a fake field goal that fell short). Bostick got Pitt into the end zone as the first half was winding down, hitting fellow freshman Maurice Williams on a 37-yard touchdown pass, and while USF scored a late field goal to cut into Pitt's lead, simply having a lead was encouraging for the Panthers.

"14-10 at halftime was terrific against that team," Bostick recalls.

The lead didn't last long. On the first play of the second half, USF quarterback Matt Grothe, whose mobility tortured plenty of Big East teams over the course of his career, faked a pass to the right and then turned and ran to his left, where there were no Pitt defenders. Grothe got into the open field and took a good angle to evade cornerback Kennard Cox, which turned a good run into a great run. Then he got a block from tight end Cedric Hill that took out three Pitt defenders, and that turned a great run into an epic touchdown run.

Grothe went 80 yards on that play, and all of a sudden, Pitt's 14-10 lead was now a 17-14 deficit. The Panthers' offense didn't have much of a response, punting on all three drives in the third quarter, but in what had become a recurring theme over the second half of the season, Pitt's defense picked up the slack.

While the offense was punting, the defense was holding South Florida in check. The Bulls scored on their first drive in the second half with the long Grothe run, but after that in the third quarter, their drives produced a fumble, a field goal and a three-and-out that led to a punt. Pitt's defense was giving up minimal points, but on the final play of the third quarter, South Florida scored another touchdown - and the Panthers' defense was on the sideline when it happened.

On first down from the Pitt 19, with three seconds left in the third quarter, Bostick dropped back and attempted a pass to tight end Darrell Strong. But USF safety Nate Allen got a better break on the pass than Strong did and picked it off, running 38 yards to the end zone to give the Bulls a 27-14 lead.

"That was a seam route and it was pretty much the beginning of the end," Bostick says, and his approximation of the events that followed is fairly accurate. Pitt punted on its first possession of the fourth quarter, and that drive was one of the Panthers' best in the final 15 minutes.

After another USF three-and-out and punt, Pitt took over on the Bulls' side of the field. But USF sent a heavy blitz at Bostick on first down; the freshman quarterback hurried a pass over the middle, and USF linebacker Ben Moffitt tipped the ball before grabbing it out of the air and taking off with an eye on the end zone.

Moffitt nearly made it; he ran 60 yards with the interception return, but he needed 62 for a touchdown. Only a tip-of-the-toes tackle by Pitt running back LaRod Stephens-Howling kept the USF linebacker from crossing the goal line. But it didn't matter; USF's offense got those final two yards it needed for the score over the course of the next three plays.

Pitt was down 34-14, a 20-point deficit that seemed pretty tough to overcome with less than ten minutes left in the game, but the Panthers' defense kept fighting and forced another USF punt to give the offense another shot. And as the fourth quarter started turning into a wild affair, Pitt's offense finally answered the bell, driving 75 yards in seven plays with Bostick completing all five of his pass attempts before McCoy ran into the end zone from 12 yards out to cut the lead to 13.

The Panthers attempted an onside kick after the touchdown, hoping recover it for a chance at a quick score, but South Florida recovered it. With the way the defense was playing, though, that failed kick attempt just meant Pitt's offense had to wait an extra 90 seconds before getting the ball back, as Scott McKillop and the rest of his teammates on defense forced another three-and-out – the third of the second half – and put the offense back on the field.

But if Pitt's defense shutting down the USF offense was a theme of the second half, so was this: USF's defense catching one of Bostick's passes. On the first play of the next drive after the punt, it happened again. Bostick tried a pass to receiver TJ Porter, but he focused in on Porter too much, allowing USF defensive back Trae Williams to read his eyes and make a jump on the pass.

Williams caught the interception at the 21-yard line and trotted into the end zone. It was South Florida's third interception of the day and the second one that was taken directly across the goal line (remember, Moffitt was tackled at the 2 after his pick).

Pitt wasn't entirely deflated by the second pick-six; in fact, the Panthers scored two more touchdowns before the game was over, including McCoy's third rushing touchdown of the day. That score gave the freshman running back 14 rushing touchdowns on the season, breaking Tony Dorsett's 34-year Pitt record for rushing touchdowns as a freshman.

But the damage was done. The three interceptions had eliminated Pitt's chances of winning, overshadowing another stellar defensive performance – the defense had really only given up three touchdowns while holding the Bulls to 352 yards, which was well below their season average of 427.9 yards per game to that point.

USF came into Heinz Field with its offense on a roll, topping 440 yards in each of the four games leading up to the game against Pitt. But the Panthers' defense was better that day, as it had been for just about every game in the second half of the season.

Since the loss to Navy, which saw the Midshipmen put up a gaudy 497 yards of total offense, Pitt had held every opponent to 358 yards or less. USF had finished the day with 48 points, but 21 of those came directly from turnovers, and the remaining 27 represented the first time since the Navy game that Pitt's defense had allowed more than 24 points in a game.

Week after week, the strong defense had been undone by an unreliable, inconsistent and ineffective offense. Despite having a generational talent in LeSean McCoy, Pitt's offense couldn't sustain any kind of consistent attack because it couldn't sustain any kind of consistent passing attack.

For Wannstedt, it was his deepest fears realized.

"My tolerance for quarterbacks – I'd probably still be coaching at Chicago and at the Dolphins and at Pitt if I had a little bit more tolerance for quarterbacks," he says. "But for some reason, I was just convinced that we could win a national championship or a Super Bowl running the ball, playing defense, as long as the quarterback didn't screw it up. And the minute that the quarterback screwed something up – by that I mean, made a bad decision or threw an interception – my coaches used to laugh because everybody knew what was coming: 'That's it, I've seen enough, Wildcat, get the ball to Shady. I don't care if we throw another pass.'

"When you look at those games, that's pretty much what happened. It was kind of halfway comical, but that was a little bit of hardheadedness, I guess."

To a man, though, players and coaches from that team say that there was never any issue between the offense and the defense, never anyone on the successful side looking down on the other side. The team was a team; they won as a team and lost as one, too.

"That's how football goes, and I'll be honest with you: that entire season, there was nobody pointing fingers," says McKillop, who had 18 tackles in the loss to South Florida. "I know that's the easiest thing to do: when the offense does well or the defense does well, it's easy to point fingers. I think that speaks volumes about Coach Wannstedt that we trusted, we believed. Maybe we didn't win, we didn't come out on the scoresheet, but we had the most faith, no matter who they put out there at quarterback."

"Our players were unbelievable," Wannstedt says. "They were so confident in the plan that we had and the way we were going about it. Everything was the way it should be: we had young players and they were working hard and we were out recruiting hard and we were trying to build a program. I had great support at that time from the administration. Was I frustrated and felt like punching my fist through the wall? Absolutely. But it never showed on the field and it never showed with the players because they were working so hard."

It was a season-long process for the team and especially for the defense, which had gone from getting gashed by Navy's triple-option offense to being the backbone of the squad. The young defensive linemen had grown up, McKillop was playing at an all-conference level, and the unit as a whole had become formidable. The year before, Pitt's defense had featured NFL-caliber stars like Darrelle Revis and H.B. Blades and Clint Session and had struggled; in 2007, with those big-name players gone, the defense turned a page.

"They were a lot of fun to coach," Paul Rhoads says. "If you went back and pulled out, I don't know, the last 40 years or back to the national championship era of Pitt and looked at all the teams that had great defenses and looked at the players on those teams compared to the players on that team, that team's going to be down towards the bottom.

"But overall, they were just tough as hell. Early in our tenure there, we played with some guys like Gerald Hayes and Lew Moore and Revis; we had some good players and had some good defenses. But that group, I didn't expect to finish the way they did. But when we got hot, we got hot. They had a confidence that if they played together, they could stop anybody. And they proved that to the end of the season."

THOSE DARN PANTHERS

There was no denying what was happening at the end of the season: since the start of the December 1st game at West Virginia, the Panthers had been the better team. They had given up just one touchdown to the Mountaineers' previously-unstoppable offense, an offense that was especially unstoppable when facing Pitt in the past, and they held a 10-7 lead well into the fourth quarter.

The 2007 Pitt team wasn't the same one WVU had run all over in 2005 and 2006. The 2007 Pitt team had a defensive line that could collapse the pocket and a middle linebacker that didn't miss tackles and a half-dozen or so other linebackers and defensive backs and linemen who had learned, over the course of a difficult and challenging season, how good they could be.

They were beating West Virginia, and there were no excuses: no bad calls or weather or any other place where blame could be assigned. Pitt was controlling West Virginia, and the only possible caveat WVU fans could fall back on was that the Mountaineers had been playing since the middle of the second quarter without their best player, quarterback Pat White.

That was the Mountaineer' lone excuse, and when ESPN returned from a commercial break with eight minutes left in the game, that lone excuse turned into a lone hope, as White, with his injured right thumb, was warming up on the sidelines.

Television cameras even captured him telling team trainers, "I'm fine."

The West Virginia fans noticed White throwing on the sidelines, and when the Mountaineers' offense took the field after a Pitt field goal made the score 13-7, the crowd erupted at the site of No. 5 running out to the line of scrimmage.

White was back, and the fans were certain WVU's fortunes would change.

Naturally, Rich Rodriguez dialed up a run for White on his first play back, and the salvation of White's return was promptly stymied when Pitt linebackers Scott McKillop and Jemeel Brady dropped the WVU quarterback for no gain.

Running back Steve Slaton picked up five yards on a second-down run, but White's run on third-and-5 gained just two, putting the Mountaineers in a fourth-down situation. Despite the short gains on those three plays, WVU was in Pitt territory at the 26 since Noel Devine had logged a big kickoff return after Pitt's field goal. Going for it on fourth down at that spot on the field and a six-point deficit on the scoreboard made sense.

So Rodriguez sent his offense out for the fourth-and-3 play. The game was on the line: WVU's sideline knew it, the fans in the stands definitely knew it, and Pitt's sideline knew it. Defensive coordinator Paul Rhoads, thinking back to the package he had developed to counter Rutgers' mobile quarterback, got ready for Rodriguez to put the ball in the hands of his best player.

But Rhoads also knew what White would be looking for. When White took the shotgun snap and had to decide whether to keep it and run or hand it off to Slaton, the quarterback opted to hand it off - which was exactly what Rhoads wanted him to do.

"It was an all-out blitz," Scott McKillop recalls. "We only really ran one defense the entire second half. There were different variations based on where the back was, but I just looked over to

Coach Rhoads and he kept giving me the signal: same call, same call, same call."

"It worked out well with arguably our best defender in position to make the play," Rhoads says.

True to Rhoads' words, the call worked perfectly. White read Pitt's defense after the snap and gave the ball to Slaton, who ran toward the line of scrimmage hoping to get the three yards he needed. But when he got there, McKillop was waiting for him.

Slaton only gained two of those three yards, and West Virginia turned the ball over on downs.

"It's funny because I was a pretty even-keeled player at Pitt and very rarely did I celebrate or anything; I was pretty boring," McKillop says. "And I remember, after I made it, I was like, 'Okay Scott, you have to do some sort of celebration.' All I could think of was that stupid double-fist pump or whatever, and it's funny because that's the only picture people really have."

McKillop's tackle was huge, but the game wasn't over just quite yet. Pitt's offense got the ball back with 4:05 on the clock and West Virginia holding multiple timeouts to use for stopping the clock. The Panthers went to the running game, as expected, and LeSean McCoy and Conredge Collins combined to run for six yards on two plays, setting up a third-and-4 that was looking like it could be the biggest play of the game.

Dave Wannstedt and Matt Cavanaugh stuck with the run game on third down, as quarterback Pat Bostick faked a handoff to Collins and then pitched the ball to McCoy, who ran for seven yards to pick up a first down and get Pitt that much closer to victory.

But as with McCoy's earlier touchdown that got wiped out by a holding call, his seven-yard run on third-and-4 came back as well. Once again, the officials said that receiver Oderick Turner held a WVU defender on the play, and while the Pitt sideline issued its complaints, the apparent first down turned into a third-and-7.

Ironically, Bostick's incomplete pass to Turner on the subsequent third-down try seemed to hinge on WVU defensive back Antonio Lewis grabbing a fistful of Turner's jersey. That penalty did not get called, and Pitt had to punt, giving the ball back to White and the West Virginia offense one more time.

The clock ticked under three minutes when the Mountaineers' drive began, and White tried to come out throwing. A 20-yard pass to Darius Reynaud picked up a big chunk of yards for West Virginia, as did a 12-yard run by White on the next play. All of a sudden, the Mountaineers were at the Pitt 21-yard line - striking distance for a would-be game-winning touchdown.

On first down from that spot, White missed Reynaud in the end zone. Then a blitz from safety Eric Thatcher forced White to throw the ball away on second down. On third down, Rhoads dialed up another blitz; this time it was a six-man rush, and the extra rushers combined with a bobbled snap to lead to a sack by redshirt freshman defensive end Greg Romeus, a fumble that White had to scramble to recover, and a seven-yard loss.

Now, the game truly was on the line. With 1:40 on the clock, West Virginia was staring at a fourth-and-17, its last fleeting hopes of a national championship resting solely on its ability to pick up 17 yards.

Pitt sent five pass-rushers at White on fourth down, but he managed to get the pass off. It was a deep throw to the end zone, where Wes Lyons, a Pittsburgh native who turned down Pitt to attend WVU, was the intended receiver.

Pitt cornerback Jovani Chappel was covering Lyons. As both players entered the end zone with White's pass in the air, Chappel, who was in front of Lyons, slowed down just a step. That slowdown took a step off of Lyons' pace, and the ball sailed out of the end zone.

Incomplete pass. Turnover on downs. And with one minute and 34 seconds left in the game, Pitt took the ball at its own 14. The Panthers just needed to run the clock out.

Of course, Pitt should have had the ball at the 28, but after the incomplete pass, the officials called Eric Thatcher for an unsportsmanlike conduct penalty. Thatcher had, in the view of the officials, extended his middle finger to the crowd while he was celebrating the incomplete pass on fourth down.

On the sideline, Wannstedt was irate with Thatcher, who tried to plead his case, pointing out that the index finger and middle finger on his left hand were taped together, and that must have been what the officials saw.

Nevertheless, Pitt was close. The win was close. Redemption and an unbelievably-fitting end to a season full of challenges, full of adversity - it was all in Pitt's grasp. The Panthers just needed to kill 94 seconds of clock.

The next three plays were just about what most would expect. McCoy ran the ball three times and gained a net of one yard (really, he gained six yards, but Pitt lost five yards on third-and-7 when the Panthers, in true 2007 fashion, took a delay of game penalty on third down).

But the play that mattered most, the one that truly counted, was on fourth-and-9. Pitt's punt team took the field and snapped the ball to punter Dave Brytus with four seconds on the clock. Brytus caught the snap, turned around, and ran into the end zone. He headed for the back line and then ran along it, waiting just long enough for those final four seconds to tick away before he stepped out of bounds, taking a safety that ended the game.

4...3...2...1...Final.

"I could not have anticipated the result. At all," Bostick says 10 years later. "Being transparent, I personally wanted to go down there and play solid and not lose the game for us, hopefully heading to the offseason making sense of the whole year for myself."

Bostick threw for 67 yards and two interceptions that night in Morgantown, but he also rushed for the Panthers' lone touchdown. McCoy had put in a hero's effort, carrying the ball 38 times for 148 yards. Meanwhile, Pitt's defense had held West Virginia to just 183 yards of total offense (42 yards less than the Panthers produced on offense). Pat White ran for 41 yards. Steve Slaton ran for 11.

The Panthers made seven tackles for loss in the game, and those seven were spread among six different players. Four Pitt players forced a fumble. Three recovered fumbles.

"There's a couple big plays in the game," says McKillop, who led Pitt with nine tackles. "You have the big strip by Lowell Robinson. You have the fumble recovery by Tommie Duhart. You have Jemeel Brady, who was a first-time starter, playing that game because Shane Murray was a little banged up. You have a lot of things. That game, each person on defense had an opportunity to make a play and made a play.

"Every single game before that, every break went against us. That game, every break went for us."

Rich Rodriguez's postgame comments have become a thing of legend among Pitt fans.

"Golly, it was...it was just a nightmare. The whole thing was a nightmare," Rodriguez said as the sounds of the Pitt players celebrating - their locker room was next to the interview room - provided fitting ambient noise for a funereal press conference.

Rodriguez had a nightmare that night in Morgantown, but Pitt had just gone through a nightmare of a season, a chaotic and absurd three-month span that ended with a program-changing game.

"It was crazy," Bostick says. "That was the hardest year of my life. I thought, going into that game, if it went the way I thought it was going to go, you know, I still had my doubts about whether or not Pitt was - not if it Pitt was the right place for me, but if I was right for this whole thing. Because it was a whirlwind for me. But there's always a greater plan, and I think that being a part of a win like that, it redirected my mind to trust what my heart had told me all along:

"That Pitt was absolutely the right place for me, and I wanted to be a part of something really special at Pitt. In that moment, when I least expected it, I had a chance to be part of something really special in that game."

POSTGAME

10 years later, the 13-9 game still resonates.

The score alone is instantly recognizable among Pitt fans. It's an unconventional score, of course, produced as it was by two touchdowns, two field goals, and a safety. But for the fans who were in Morgantown that night or were watching on television or have simply been told about it years later, it immediately conjures memories of the time Pitt faced its bitter foes in a game that no one thought it could win.

It's really not hyperbole. As clichéd as it sounds, the only people who believed Pitt could beat West Virginia were in Pitt's locker room. It simply defied all logic and reason.

And to be fair to just about everyone who expected a WVU win, that logic and reason were well-founded. There were signs of improvement with the Panthers over the course of the 2007 season, but the team really had no business being in the game with West Virginia, which probably made the win mean that much more.

That's why it was important to tell not just the story of the 13-9 game but the season as a whole. It occurred to me a long time ago that the season itself was the story; without the context of everything that came before it, 13-9 is just a game, just an upset.

Think about the string of events: in training camp, Pat Bostick leaves the team. In the season opener, Bill Stull gets hurt. Pitt throws away a chance at a big win against Michigan State. The

Heinz Field crowd boos the team against UConn. Dave Wannstedt tries an onside kick to open the Virginia game. Wannstedt and Matt Cavanaugh try to throw from the 2 against Navy. Pitt pulls its first upset of the season - in a game that gets overlooked, even though it stands as one of Wannstedt's best wins - to beat Cincinnati. Bostick and LeSean McCoy fumble at Louisville. A terrible offensive pass interference call costs them the game at Rutgers. The defense plays great against South Florida but Bostick throws basically three touchdowns to the Bulls.

And then, in the most improbable, most bizarre twist of them all, that 4-7 Pitt team that couldn't get out of its own way, that couldn't buy a bit of good luck, goes to Morgantown and owns the Mountaineers.

It's almost too Hollywood.

Of course, since that game, Pitt has pulled a couple more classic upsets. Nine years after 13-9, the Panthers, with Pat Narduzzi as their head coach, headed to face an undefeated Clemson team that was ranked No. 2 in the country, and they pulled out a win on a last-second field goal.

A year after that, with similarities that were not missed by anyone, a 4-7 Pitt team faced the No. 2 team in the country in the regular-season finale. This time, the Panthers were taking on Miami and the game was at home, but the result was the same:

Pitt controlled a seemingly-superior opponent for a win and a nice boost into the offseason.

The 2007 team definitely got a boost for the offseason. In the immediate aftermath of the 13-9 game, Wannstedt and his staff put together a big recruiting weekend, hosting a group of 13 prospects that included some of Pitt's top targets.

The win gave Pitt positive momentum and, perhaps most of all, some tangible evidence that what Wannstedt was doing was working. Throughout the 2007 season, the questions about

Wannstedt's likelihood of success were loud and getting louder; as each loss mounted, more and more doubts emerged about whether Wannstedt's approach to the game could work and whether Wannstedt himself was ever going to win at Pitt. The expected blowout loss to West Virginia might not have cost him his job, but it certainly would have put that job in jeopardy heading into the 2008 season.

Instead, Wannstedt went into the 2008 season with a lot of momentum. That momentum was fairly sapped when Pitt lost to Bowling Green in the 2008 opener, but the team rebounded to win 19 games in 2008 and 2009, the most successful two-year stretch for Pitt since the early 1980's.

13-9 gave everyone - players, coaches, fans, administrators (most of them, anyway) - reason to believe that the program had turned the corner.

As it went, Wannstedt's time at Pitt last three more seasons. He led the Panthers to records of 9-4, 10-3, and 7-5 before resigning - by strong suggestion from Athletic Director Steve Pederson and Chancellor Mark Nordenberg - at the end of the 2010 regular season. Wannstedt kicked around the NFL as an assistant coach for the next three years, including one year as a special teams coach on Greg Schiano's staff with the Tampa Bay Buccaneers. Once he hung up the proverbial whistle, Wannstedt settled into a nice career as a football analyst.

Paul Rhoads left Pitt after the 2007 season to serve as defensive coordinator at Auburn, where he stayed for a year before becoming the head coach at Iowa State. In 2017, he was the defensive coordinator at Arkansas.

Scott McKillop took his outstanding 2007 season and turned it into an even better 2008. As a redshirt senior he made 137 tackles, 17.5 tackles for loss, four sacks, and two interceptions on his way to being named Big East Defensive Player of the Year. After a short stint in the NFL, McKillop followed the path most expected for him and moved into coaching.

Pat Bostick played at Pitt for four seasons. He started one more game in his career after the 2007 season, replacing Bill Stull for a game at Notre Dame in 2008 that ended memorably with Pitt winning in four overtimes. He eventually decided to retire from football after Wannstedt's departure following the 2010 season, but he was never far from Pitt. In 2011, he became the color commentator on Pitt's radio broadcasts, a role he held for five years before he stepped down to take on a larger position in the Athletic Department. In 2017, he was named the Associate Athletic Director for Major Gifts.

On the other side of the equation, Rich Rodriguez never got to take West Virginia to a national championship. Less than two weeks after losing to Pitt in 2007, he left the Mountaineers to become the head coach at Michigan.

He was one of quite a few voices I wish could have contributed to this project; not surprisingly, he wasn't too interested in opining on a game that is 10 years old but probably still stings like it was yesterday.

There were a lot of other people I would have liked to hear from on the topic of the 13-9 game and Pitt's 2007 season. Pat White is one of them; I would have liked to get his thoughts and reflections on that game. For now, we'll have get by with a tweet he sent as the 2016 Panthers were upsetting No. 2 Clemson, a game that seemed to strike a little too close to home for the former WVU standout:

"Those darn Panthers"

ACKNOWLEDGMENTS

This book would not have been possible without the invaluable contributions of Dave Wannstedt, Paul Rhoads, Pat Bostick, and Scott McKillop. All four of those individuals were more than giving with their time, answering a lot of questions from me as I asked them to recall the specifics of events that happened 10 years ago. For their anecdotes, recollections, and reflections on the circumstances surrounding that unbelievable season, I can't thank them enough.

Also, thanks to Zach Lantz, who designed the cover of this book, and to Pete Madia for providing the photos for the cover.

Finally, thanks to the Pitt fans whose passion and love for the Panthers - as challenging as it may be at times - convinced me that there were people who would want to read about a decade-old football season.

ABOUT THE AUTHOR

Chris Peak has been a writer for Panther-Lair.com since 2005, covering Pitt football, basketball, and recruiting for the Rivals.com network. He graduated from Pitt with a degree in English literature in 2001 or 2002 (depending on the paperwork). He currently lives in Mt. Lebanon, a South Hills suburb of Pittsburgh, with his wife and two sons.

Made in the USA
Coppell, TX
30 April 2020